Family History Documentation Guidelines

Second Edition

Silicon Valley PAF Users Group

www.svpafug.org

Copyright Restrictions

Acknowledgements

Ordering Informatio.On

Copyright Restrictions

Acknowledgements

The *Family History Documentation Guidelines* was developed and produced by a committee designated by the board of the Silicon Valley PAF Users Group. The second edition was prepared by Mary Lou Harline, Lesly Klippel, and Richard Rands*. Janet Brigham Rands was the editor.

These guidelines have been widely accepted as a universal standard for all family history databases programs. It is essential that all family history documentation be thorough and consistent, and the guidelines specified in this book will provide a basis for a worldwide standard. The guidelines and examples in this booklet are based on the scheme for documenting sources and notes in Personal Ancestral File (PAF) versions 3, 4, and 5. It is our understanding that documentation methodology in the future will not change appreciably. Since researchers share information using a variety of different software programs, many of which use methods similar to the PAF scheme, it is our hope that these guidelines will be universal enough for general acceptance.

*Contributors to the first edition were:
Richard Halliday
Mary Lou Harline
Lesly Klippel
Alice Malquist
Leland Osburn
Richard Rands
Richard Simonsen

Ordering Information

Copies of this book may be ordered from the web page at:

www.svpafug.org

or by mail from:

Silicon Valley PAF Users Group
P.O. Box 23670, San Jose, CA 95153-3670, USA.

For prices and bulk discount rates, please see the web page listed above.

ISBN 0-9704156-0-5

Table of Contents

Trademarks

Permissions

User Group Membership

Downloading PAF

Printing History

Trademarks

FamilySearch® is a trademark of Intellectual Reserve, Inc., Salt Lake City, Utah. Macintosh® is a registered trademark of Apple Computer Corporation, Cupertino, California.

Permissions and Copyrights

Some material in this publication is reprinted by permission of The Church of Jesus Christ of Latter-day Saints. In granting permission for this use of copyrighted material, the Church does not imply or express either endorsement or authorization of this publication.

Membership Information

Join the Silicon Valley PAF Users Group at:

www.svpafug.org

The Silicon Valley PAF Users Group is a nonprofit organization intended to promote the use of computer software for genealogy research.

Membership entitles you to *PAFinder*, a widely acclaimed newsletter published each month there is a meeting. Meetings are held monthly, except December, every second Saturday, from 9 to 11 a. m., at The Church of Jesus Christ of Latter-day Saints, 875 Quince Ave. Santa Clara, California.

Membership fees are $15 per year ($20 for Canada, $25 other international). Application for membership is available on the web site at:

www.svpafug.org

or by mail at:

SV-PAF-UG
P.O. Box 23670,
San Jose, CA 95153-3670 USA.

Downloading the PAF for Windows Program

PAF 5 is free on the Internet. PAF 3 may be ordered through the LDS Church for $15.00, and upgrades are available for free on the Web.

PAF versions 4 and 5, and the upgrade to version 3 can be downloaded free of charge from the Internet at:

www.familysearch.org

Click on *Order Family History Resources, Software Downloads—Free*, and click on the desired version. Save the downloaded file and then run it from *Start, Run.*

Printing History

Edition 1, July 2000

Edition 2, January 2003

Introduction

Much has changed in the world of computer-aided genealogy database software since the Silicon Valley PAF Users Group first published its documentation guidelines in 1992. Not only have new versions of the Personal Ancestral File (PAF) program been released, but several alternative programs have become popular among genealogists and family historians. Furthermore, all of the systems have more sophisticated methods for entering and maintaining documentation. In addition, the cost of hard disk memory space has plummeted, thus making it far more feasible to include as part of your database more detailed documentation, as well as digital copies of photos, certificates, and other source documents.

Beginning with PAF 4, the software is a Windows-based program.

The second edition of the guidelines has been updated to reflect PAF version 5 and subsequent versions, plus other programs that separate source citations from notes. Since the documentation method in PAF version 3 and version 4 is similar, many of these guidelines also will apply to those who are using those versions.

This new edition is aimed at PAF versions 4 and 5. See Chapter Seven for help with PAF 3.

For those who are just starting to enter documentation, the major change from the earlier versions is in the use of templates for sources, in place of a free-form or blank screen. Notes still may be entered in the free-form notes screen, but the details of sources are now entered into a separate formatted template.

The goal of the committee has not changed since the original guidelines were published in 1992. We still believe that good documentation is an essential element of genealogical data. We feel strongly that documentation should be consistent, clear, and thorough. The primary objective is to describe the source of data in such a way that anyone who desires can return to the source if there is ever a need to verify the information or to resolve conflicts in the data.

Good documentation is consistent, clear, and thorough.

How to Use This Manual

This manual is designed to be a supplement to the user documentation of the program you are using for your database. PAF users not familiar with PAF for Windows will need to review the overall functionality of the program using a PAF manual or the Help text supplied by the Family History Department of the LDS Church. *Family History Documentation Guidelines* is intended to establish a method for good, consistent source documentation regardless of the software you use.

A few sections in this manual contain how-to instructions that will be helpful for users who want more extensive instructions on using the PAF 4

Experienced users can skip the how-to sections.

and PAF 5 source documentation features. However, if you are already familiar with these features, you may want to skip the how-to chapters and go directly to the guidelines and examples.

If you are just beginning to document your family history, we hope you will study the guidelines carefully to try understand the overall method we are recommending. Those who are already deep into source documentation and have some experience in the functionality of the PAF 4 and 5 system will note that the method described herein has several major elements.

Use clear and consistent source titles.

First, we are suggesting that great care be made when entering the source title in the Source template. If you do not use a clear and consistent format for source titles, your Source List will be difficult to use and you will be more apt to have needless duplications. The whole purpose of the source system will be defeated, and you will be frustrated. Chapter 3 will be especially helpful for understanding source title entries.

Use sources and notes wisely.

Second, we are recommending that care be made when choosing to put information into the Source and Citation screens, as opposed to putting it into the Notes screen. While we recognize that this is a personal preference, and although the PAF system allows for many *Other Events* to be created for source documentation, we hope you will notice that too many source entries can clutter the Source List.

Source titles should reflect the type of document or the geographical area covered.

Finally, we suggest that your source titles describe the type of source material, such as the kind of document or publication media. However, some situations could favor using a surname to indicate the branch of the family, or a geographical format in a title that indicates the region that the source document covers.

Menus, buttons, options, and keys are *italicized* in this manual.

We use style conventions in this manual to indicate specific functions. Usually titles of menus, buttons, options, or keys that you must press or click are *italicized*. Other labels or menus that appear on the screens or windows are capitalized. Many of the common terms for computer use have been placed in the Glossary.

Please send the committee your comments and suggestions.

As was the case for the previous edition, these guidelines are not endorsed by anyone other than the Silicon Valley PAF Users Group. The committee has spent many hours working out the details to ensure that the guidelines will be highly useful and widely accepted. We continue to seek comments and suggestions for improvement. Please feel free to send them to this address:

Documentation Committee
P.O. Box 23670
San Jose, CA 95153-3670 USA

or e-mail them to: guidelines@svpafug.org

Glossary and Abbreviations

Abbreviations in documentation should be minimized, or avoided altogether. Below are many common English abbreviations, computer terms, and acronyms encountered in genealogy research and software.

abt	about
AF	Ancestral File
AFN	ancestral file number
aka	also known as
Alt	*Alt* (alternate) key on a computer keyboard
Amer	America
Ancestral File	lineage-linked database maintained by the LDS Church
ANSI, ANSEL, ASCII	common code formats used for storing data in computer files
appurtenance	something belonging to something else, as in buildings belonging to a manor
argent	silver or white color, in heraldry
assize	a court hearing
azure	blue color, in heraldry
b	born
backslash	the "\" character on a computer keyboard
backup	process to archive a database files for long-term storage
bapt	baptized
banns	legally required announcement of intent to marry
BBS	bulletin board system
browser	program for accessing the World Wide Web and the Internet
BT	bishop's transcript
bur	buried
c, ca, circ	circa, about
calc	calculated
cartulary	a compilation of land records
CD-ROM	compact disk with read-only data
cem	cemetery
cert	certificate
chevage	a fee for permission to live away from one's lord
chr	christening
chron	chronological
circa	about, of, or approximately
Co.,co.	county
cod	codex
col	column, colony, colonial
coparceners	co-heirs
corresp.	correspondence
ctl, ctrl	*Ctrl* (control) key on a computer keyboard
crem	cremated
curtilage	area of land surrounding a house
custumal	a detailed survey of property and services owed to a manor lord
d	died
DDR	Dead Duty Register
dec	decree, deceased
demesne	land of a manor retained by the lord
dept	department
diacritic	mark added to a letter to specify a phonetic value or to distinguish otherwise identical words
dialog box	window containing field for entering information into a program
differencing	slight variations in a coat of arms to distinguish between heirs
dist	district

Glossary and Abbreviations

abt — dist

The meaning of an abbreviation changes over time, leading to confusion or misunderstanding, especially when encountered by someone whose native language differs from that of the person who recorded the abbreviation.

Glossary and Abbreviations

You often will find the abbreviation *Do* or *do* in census records following an individual's given name. This means the individual's surname is the same as that of the person listed above the abbreviation.

The abbreviation *inst* is sometimes used in dates when the current month is specified elsewhere and should be clear to the reader.

Do, do	ditto, same as above
d.s.p.	died without children
dtd	dated
E.D.	enumeration district
ed	editor, edition, edited
edn	edition
EIC	East India Company
eol	end of line, computer code used to specify the Enter key on a computer keyboard
ESC	*Esc* (escape) key on a computer keyboard
enfeoffment	process of transferring property to a new tenant
ermine	background pattern of fur, in heraldry
escutcheon of pretense	portion of a wife's coat of arms added to a man's coat of arms
estreat	a list of tenants owing fines to a lord
et ux	*et uxor*, Latin: and wife
eyre	early English court hearing
fam	family
FamilySearch®	LDS software program and Web site for searching family history; see www.familysearch.org
feu, sub-feu	Scottish system of land grants
FFHS	Federation of Family History Societies
FGS	Federation of Genealogical Societies
FHC	Family History Center
FHL	Family History Library, Salt Lake City, Utah
FHLC	Family History Library Catalog
filter	instructions to limit the data being selected
forward slash	the "/" character on a computer keyboard
FRC	Family Records Center, London, England
GEDCOM	file format for exchanging genealogy data between databases
glebe terrier	a survey of parish church possessions
Google	popular Internet search engine
GRO	General Register Office, Kew, England
GSU	Genealogical Society of Utah
gules	red color, in heraldry
hist soc	historical society
heriot	a list of fines on new tenants of a manor
hosp	hospital
HTML	hypertext markup language; for formatting Web pages
IGI	International Genealogical Index
ILL	Inter-library loan
infefment	Scottish process of transferring property to a new tenant
info	information
inst	this month
Int. Dec.	interlocutory decree
intestate	dying without making a will, or with a will that does not pass probate
ISP	Internet service provider; provides access to the Internet
LDS	Latter-day Saints, abbr. for The Church of Jesus Christ of Latter-day Saints
LC, LOC	Library of Congress
Levee en Masse	military enlistment records
LH	left-hand (page)
libr	library
m, marr, md	married, marriage

Many of the terms in these pages are used in wills and- descriptions of coats of arms.

manumission	the procedure of buying freedom from servitude
media	material or device containing data
mem	memorial
menu bar	bar with menu labels at the top of a Windows or Macintosh screen
merchet	a lord's fee for permission for a servant's daughter to marry
messuage	a dwelling house
moiety	half share of an estate
mos	months
MRIN	marriage record identification number
multimedia	files containing graphics, photos, sound, or movies (see Table A-6)
NEHGS	New England Historic Genealogical Society
NGS	National Genealogical Society
nil	no information located
non-conformist	A religious group of dissenters from the Anglican church
obit	obituary
OI	Ordinance Index
ONS	Office for National Statistics, Kew, England
OPR	Old Parochial Records for Scotland
or	gold or yellow color, in heraldry
orig	original
p, pg, pgs	page, pages
PAF	Personal Ancestral File
PCC	Prerogative Court of Canterbury
PCY	Prerogative Court of York
pop-up window	box on computer screen providing or requiring information
poss	possession
Posse Comitatus	record of military enlistments
pp, ppg	pages
prepd	prepared
PRF	Pedigree Resource File, collection of family history files submitted to the Family History Library through the Internet
PRO	Public Records Office, Kew, England
prob	probably
probate	the process of proving a will or evidence validating a will
Pts	*in partibus transmarinis*, Latin: in countries overseas, abroad
pubr	publisher
publ	published
pull-down menu	Windows or Macintosh menu accessed by clicking on a menu's label
purpure	purple color, in heraldry
R.D.	registration district
rec	record
regnal year	dating system based on the period of a monarch's reign
regt	regiment
relict	*relicta, relictus,* Latin: widow or widower
republ	republished
RH	right-hand (page)
RIN	record identification number
sable	black color, in heraldry
sanguine	dark red color, in heraldry
sasine	public ceremony for transferring tenancy
search engine	Internet program that facilitates searching the Web for information

Glossary and Abbreviations

scroll bar....... bar(s) in a window to bring hidden information into view

scutage.......... a payment in lieu of tenure paid by a tenant

Ser No.......... serial number

sig.................. signature

sl, sn............. *sine loco, sine nomine;* Latin: without place of publication, or without name of publication

Soc Sec......... Social Security

socage tunure ..tenure for agricultural services to a lord

sojourner...... someone who has recently moved to a new parish

soundex........ a method for coding and searching for surnames that sound alike but are spelled differently

sp.................. spouse

sps................ *sine prole supersite,* Latin: without surviving issue

SSDI............. Social Security Death Index

SSN.............. Social Security Number

status bar...... bar containing codes that indicate the state of the program

tack............... a document for a tenant's lease of land

tag................. label used in the notes screen to identify the subject of a note

task bar......... bar containing icons for launching Windows or Macintosh programs

tenne............ orange color, in heraldry

tenure........... a tenant's obligation to the land owner

template........ a form to be filled in with specific information

Temple-Ready........... program used to prepare names for submission to an LDS temple

TIB............... Temple Index Bureau

TIF............... Temple Index File

testate........... person who died with a legal will

tilde.............. (~) character on a computer keyboard

tool bar......... bar containing icons for functions available in a Windows or Macintosh program

twp............... Township

ult................. next month

UGA............. Utah Genealogical Association

UID.............. Universal ID number

Univ............. university

URL............. Uniform Resource Locator, the address of a Web site

uxor.............. Latin: a lawfully married woman

vair................ background pattern, in heraldry

virgule.......... (/) the slash, or stroke used to separate words and for parts of an Internet address

vol................. volume

wd................. will dated

Web.............. shortened term for the World Wide Web

Web site........ a specific repository of information or links to information found on the World Wide Web

wk(s)............. week(s)

wp................. will probated

ww................ will written

www............. World Wide Web

yr(s).............. year(s)

zip file.......... files that have been compressed to occupy less space or take less time to download

Task bars and tool bars are the rows of icons at the top or bottom of a computer screen that are used to perform the functions of a computer program.

Rules for Good Documentation

Rules for Good Documentation

Generic Syntax for Source Titles

Generic Syntax for Note Entries

1. Document as you go.
2. Enter sources and notes in a consistent format.
3. Enter a source description only once.
4. Use confidential information with discretion and sensitivity.
5. List all sources found for each event.
6. Identify and document conflicting or missing information.
7. Avoid using abbreviations.
8. Specify additional research where needed.
9. Strive to obtain primary sources for each event.
10. Welcome input and constructive review of your documentation.
11. Identify all researchers by name for all contributions, including your own. Use your own name, not *I* or *me*.
12. Recognize that good documentation requires continuous refinement.

A little documentation is better than none at all.

Generic Syntax for Source Titles

Method 1 (Record Type)
- Record Type: Location; Date
  - Parish Records: England, Berkshire, Reading; 1856
- Record Type: Surname; Date
  - Birth Certificate: Cox, John; 1856

Method 2 (Place Name)
- Location: Record Type; Date
  - England, Berkshire, Reading: Parish Records, 1856
- Location: Surname; Record Type; Date
  - England, Berkshire, Reading: Cox, John; Birth Certificate; 1856

Method 3 (Surname)
- Surname: Record Type; Date
  - Cox, John: Birth Certificate; 1856

Generic Syntax for Note Entries

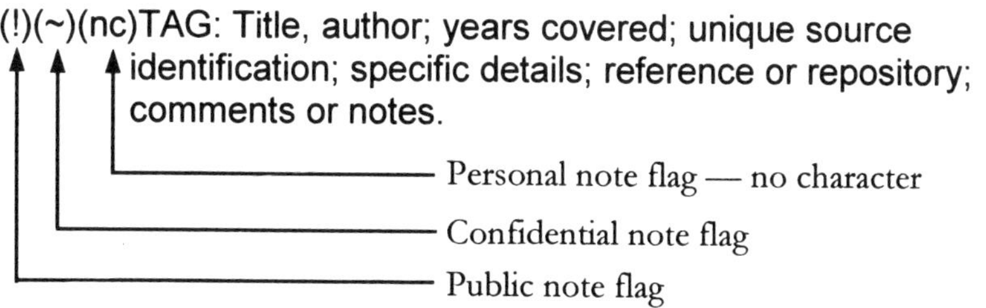

See Chapter Five for detailed instructions.

Chapter One:
Notes and Sources

What Is a Genealogy Research Source?

Chapter One: Notes and Sources

In earlier versions of PAF (before version 3) and other programs, the details about sources were entered on the same screen as notes, using a syntax similar to widely recognized footnote styles. As a result, the distinction between a source reference and a note was only in the format in which you entered them. In addition, it was necessary to repeat all the details of every source entry in every individual's record in which they were relevant.

Notes are different from sources and are entered separately.

In PAF version 3 and beyond, your source information is entered in special formatted screens that are separate from the notes screen, and you only need to enter the details of a source once. It is clearly a better method; but in order to use the system correctly, you need to understand the difference between source documentation and notes.

What Is a Genealogy Research Source?

All information comes from someplace — a source. A source could be a personal witness of an event or someone's knowledge of a family relationship. It may be an oral or written account of another witness, a book, a government-created certificate, court records, personal journals, family traditions, a conjecture about family relationships, or simply an estimate. The value or truth of the information from any source may be excellent, may have a germ of truth, or may be completely false. Some details may be documented in several sources.

Understanding the distinction between a source and a citation is important.

We casually use the term *sources* when we really mean *source citations*. A source, then, is the actual record that contains the information we use in compiling our family history. A source citation, or source description, details the information required to identify the source as a distinct, traceable record. A source citation usually provides sufficient information to allow others to discover for themselves the same information you have.

Source citations validate the accuracy of your family history.

Source details are most often included in genealogical records to authenticate the events that reveal the existence of our ancestors and their familial relationships. For example, we normally document the dates and places of births, marriages, deaths, and children or parents to prove that a person really belongs to our ancestry. These details merely form the skeleton of our family tree. We then add more details that help us to know more about who they were and how they lived. All of these details should be documented with the source of the information.

In some situations, the details about an individual do not contain a date for a birth or death. For example, a birth certificate may only indicate the names of the person's parents and not their birth dates or ages. To cover such cases, PAF includes a separate place to put an individual's nonspecific source entries that do not contain direct evidence for dates and places of a birth, marriage, or death. This feature also may be used to document the source of information that is contained in the notes.

What Is a Genealogy Research Note?

As noted above, a source citation usually is connected to an event such as a birth, christening, marriage, death, or burial, or to a family relationship. A definite time and place usually are associated with these events. Notes, on the other hand, are frequently used to give more detailed information about a person, as well as to record activities that cover a longer period of time or cover more than one place. The details of a person's education, occupation, and places he or she lived are examples of items that we call *notes.*

The nonspecific source button.

For example, the date and place of a marriage should be documented with a source citation. However, how the couple met, where they lived, how they lived, and what they accomplished are all examples of activities that are documented as notes and may or may not have a source citation. Notes also can be used to document relevant facts about the research process, such as problems with sources, conflicting data, what sources have been searched, and what still needs to be researched for an individual.

Notes often do not involve a specific date or place.

The Distinction between Sources and Notes

First, the basic, superficial, distinction between sources and notes shows on the computer screen. When you access the Notes field, you see a blank screen where you can enter any text you want to enter. When you access the Edit Sources screen, you see a template with fields where you can record the information required to identify and evaluate your source of information.

Use notes to document research activities.

PAF 4 and 5 give you the option of opening the Notes field to a screen with a default list of tags that in turn will lead to an empty screen where you can enter a new note. You can access all of the notes in a continuous display of screens or you can click on a tag that you want to access. You can create your own tags. An asterisk by the name of a tag is the signal that there are data in the Notes field with that tag.

A second distinction is not quite so clear. As has been discussed above, the Notes screen generally is to be used for biographical information, and the Source field is to be used to document where you found the information for an individual. The source citation is necessary so that you or someone else can find the origin of your information, for further study.

Sources and Notes are printed differently on reports.

Use the same source entry over and over again for every event it covers.

The third distinction between notes and sources in PAF 4 and 5 is how they are printed on the Family Group Records and Individual Summary reports. PAF 4 and 5 print the sources as footnotes with superscripted referral numbers; notes are printed as in earlier versions, following the standard entry for all the children, first giving any notes for the marriage (which also can include information about a divorce) and then giving the notes for each child.

PAF 3 still prints the sources preceding the notes, with the sources and notes for the marriage printing after the children's data, followed by the sources and notes for each child.

A fourth distinction is that source entries are reusable. While you can use the Edit function in the Notes screen to "copy and paste" information from one note to another, each source citation is accessed from a separate Source List and can be used for other individuals and events without retyping or copying. For instance, a death certificate may be the source of information for death, burial, birth, and family information. The source description is created once and is then accessed again and again through the source list each time it is to be linked as the source citation for subsequent events.

Evaluation of Sources

The Need for Evaluating Sources

Every family history depends upon sources to document its data. Data has become readily available from sources such as books, microfilms, microfiche, CDs, e-mail messages, Web sites on the Internet, and a variety of unpublished documents. A comparison of the data from these sources sometimes results in a discrepancy in the information such as the date or place of an event, the parentage of an ancestor, or even which persons really belong as children in a family. It is necessary for the researcher to understand how to evaluate sources and arrive at a conclusion about what actually is the truth.

Legal Criteria

The United States court system has two criteria for making a decision on a case before the court. A criminal case is decided by finding enough evidence to prove the case beyond a reasonable doubt. A civil case is decided by the preponderance of evidence. Genealogists also have used the term *preponderance of evidence,* since it is rare that enough evidence can be produced to "prove a case" in family history "beyond reasonable doubt." However, *preponderance of evidence* must be used with caution in today's world, since technology has made possible the proliferation of a large amount of unsubstantiated data. Repeating unreliable conclusions does not make them factual. Errors such as transpositions in dates, names of places that did not exist at the time of an event, and incorrect placement of children in families appear in many sources.

The Researcher's Responsibility

Avoid creating "junk genealogy."

There is no standard in family history research. Each researcher is a law unto himself — the judge and the jury — and researchers have varying degrees of capability and accuracy. As a result, you must evaluate data very carefully and solve any discrepancies to create a factual history of your family and avoid creating "junk genealogy." Following are some guidelines to help you become a skilled and competent family history researcher

Classification of Information

Types of evidence

Primary evidence is recorded at or near the time of the event by someone with personal knowledge of the facts or someone authorized to record the facts. An original record with primary evidence is generally accepted as the most reliable type of record if it is clearly readable. A photocopy or electronic image of an original record, or an official or certified copy of an original record, usually is considered to be as reliable as the original record. Although there is a possibility of error in reproducing an original record, it is generally minimal.

Secondary evidence is recorded after the fact and is also called *hearsay*. The truth of secondary evidence depends upon the knowledge of the informant. Mistakes can be made under the stress of certain events, and memories cannot always be relied upon. Even family Bibles have been found to contain many errors in dates when compared to original parish registers that recorded the same events. Many records, such as death certificates, contain both primary and secondary evidence.

Primary and secondary evidence can be classified further as direct or indirect. Direct evidence gives a direct answer to a question about an event or relationship. For example, an individual's birth certificate contains direct, primary evidence of the date and place of birth, although a birth date on a death certificate can be considered as direct secondary evidence. It answers the question about the birth but was recorded long after the fact by an informant who may or may not have known the correct date.

Indirect (or circumstantial) evidence implies an answer but requires some deduction or reasoning before a conclusion can be reached. For example, a census gives an age that implies a year of birth. The fact that a daughter's name is not included in her father's will provides circumstantial evidence that she died before her father. Circumstantial evidence provides clues that should be followed up by further research in other sources.

Abstracts and Transcriptions

An abstract or summary is a brief statement of what the abstractor considered to be the most important genealogical information. For example, will and deed abstracts include any dates, places, names, and relationships as mentioned in the will or deed. Since there is a chance for error in making an abstract, it should be considered as an index, and the original record should be reviewed. However, when an abstract is the only document available, use it as your source citation, but make sure to indicate that it is an abstract.

A transcription is a word-for-word copy of the original record, or a translation from another language, and its accuracy depends upon the skill of the transcriber or translator. Again, it is best to view the original record, if possible. Always indicate in your source citation that the record is transcribed or translated.

An abridgement is a shortened version of a record, which includes the basic contents. For example, an abridgement of a deed may leave out the standard legal phrases but include the names, dates, and description of the property.

As you collect genealogical information, there are some important questions to be considered:

- How close to the time of the event was the record made?
- How competent was the witness or the recorder of the event?
- Is the information logical and consistent with other known facts?
- Is the information consistent with the customs of the times?
- If the source is a compiled work, does it give sources for the information?

Remember that appearance of data in a book, on a microfilm, or in living color on a computer screen does not necessarily make it true. Each record must be evaluated for reliability and accuracy.

Quality of evidence is more important than quantity of evidence. With today's computers and the Internet, information can be disseminated many times very quickly to many researchers. Therefore, bad information from unreliable sources is too readily available. A wise researcher will strive to locate primary, direct evidence to substantiate the claims in any compiled or secondary source.

Quality of evidence is more important than quantity of evidence.

Conflicts in Data

Different records for the same event will sometimes contain conflicting information. Resolving conflicts in data requires careful research and consideration of the quality of the sources cited. In genealogical research, as in the criminal court system, a "rush to judgment" or a preconceived opinion can result in a flawed conclusion. Keeping an open mind is a requirement for both a member of a jury and a genealogical researcher.

While a court decision may be final, a genealogical record can and should be changed if new evidence is found. Unfortunately, it is sometimes necessary to admit that there is no solution to a problem and that your premise is based on an examination of the available data and a lack of conflicting evidence. Any conclusions you make should be carefully and completely recorded in the Notes screen of the individuals involved, so that future researchers can benefit from and avoid repeating your detective work.

Some Definitions

Document — A written account of an event, frequently originated by a civil or ecclesiastical agency.

Documentation — A record of the sources used to compile the events in the life of an individual as well as family relationships. This is also called "citing the sources."

Documenting events in a person's life — For a living person, this may mean recording the events in a person's life from informal records or individual memory without the use of a strict record of the sources of the information.

Evidence — Information, including records, objects, testimony of witnesses, intended to substantiate claims.

Fact — Truth known by observation or actual experience; actual or alleged event.

Information — Facts concerning dates and places of events in the life of an individual as well as family relationships.

Proof — Accumulation of enough evidence to establish the information as being true or reliable.

Record — Preserved knowledge of facts and events.

Repository — Physical location of a document, records, or other information.

Source — Documents, records, books, and information in other media from which we get information.

Source Citation — Description of the source sufficient to allow a person to access it.

Chapter Two:

How to Create Sources

Creating a New Source Citation

Chapter Two: How to Create Sources

Creating a New Source Citation

Normally, you will add a new source entry while entering or editing the information for an individual. When working on the information of an individual, you must have the Edit Individual window showing on the screen as shown below.

The Edit Individual window in PAF 5

Double click on the Source selector buttons to access the Edit Source template.

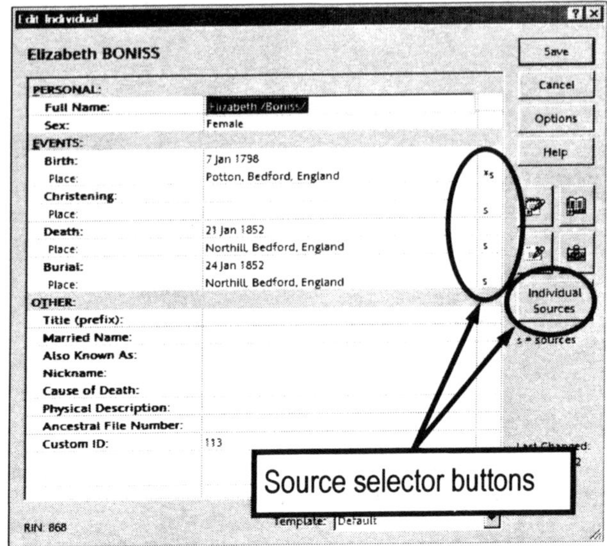

Source selector buttons — From the Edit Individual window, double-click on the Source selector button (*s*) to the right of the event to which you wish to link a source. If your source does not apply to a specific event, click on the *Individual Source* button in the right margin of the window. An empty Select Sources window will appear as shown here.

The Select Sources window

Note: All screen images in these guidelines, except for those in Chapter 7, are illustrations from PAF 5.

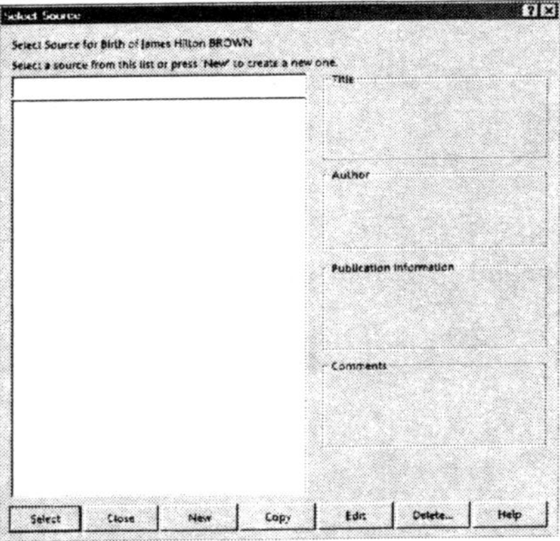

***New* Button** — Click the *New* button at the bottom of the window.

Source Title field — The Edit Source template appears as shown below with the cursor in the Source Title field. Type the source title of your source document and press *Tab*. Do not press *Enter*, as this will close the window. See Chapter Three for guidelines for entering the items in the source template.

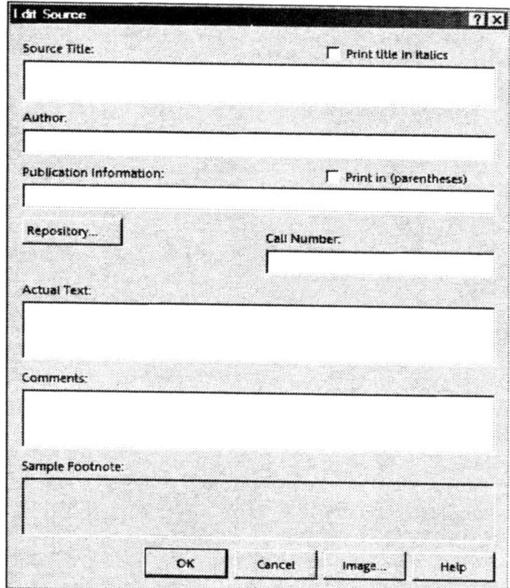

Author field — Type the name of the author and press *Tab*. The author's last name should be entered first.

Publication Information Field — Enter any publication information including place of publishing, publisher's name, and the copyright date.

Repository Button — Click on the *Repository* button. The Select Repository window appears as shown below. Click on the *Add* button at the bottom of the window to add a new repository.

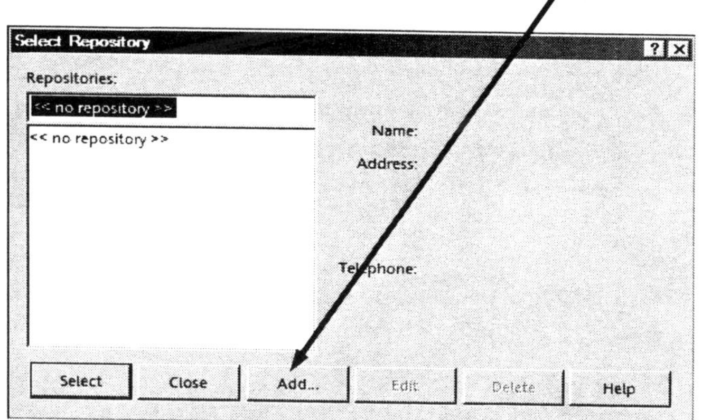

The Edit Source template

Use the tab key on your keyboard (⭾) to move the curser to the next field.

The Select Repository window

Chapter Two: How to Create Sources

Creating a New Source Citation

The Repository window

In the Repository window, type the name, address and telephone number of the facility or location that houses the record. If the item is in possession of a person, obtain that person's permission before entering an address, telephone number, and E-mail address. Click on the *OK* button when you have completed the form.

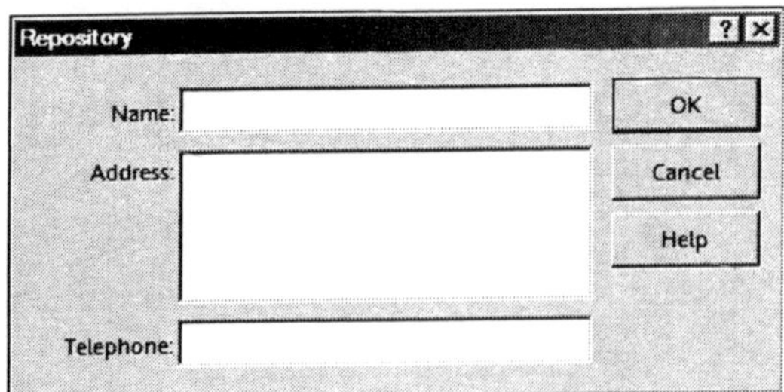

The Repository List will reappear. Highlight the repository you just entered, click the *Select* button and press *Tab*. You may also double-click on the repository you just entered.

Call Number — Back on the Edit Source template, enter the call number for the source, if applicable. Do not include information specific to the event citation, but rather use information for the source as a whole.

Annotations to the actual text should be enclosed in square brackets: [ ]

Actual Text — Enter any actual text that applies to the source as a whole. Quotation marks are automatically added to the text when printing.

Comments — Make any applicable comments about the document, such as "Bad microfilm copy" or "Entire record is very legible."

Decide if you want the title printed in italics or the publication information printed in parentheses. Book titles, most published works (for example, periodical titles, newspaper titles, or journal titles), and names of ships should be printed in italics. Publication information should be enclosed in parentheses when the citation is to be printed as a footnote. If either of these cases exist, check the appropriate box on the template. The footnote appearing at the bottom of the screen shows the way it will print out on charts, reports and in books.

In PAF 4, italics in the sample footnote will be designated by codes instead of italic font. In PAF 5 it will be displayed in italics.

If the footnote appears the way you want it, click the *OK* button to complete the source entry. The Select Source window will reappear with the new Source entry located in the alphabetical location of the list based on the Source Title, and it will be highlighted. Click on the *Select* button. You can also double-click on the source entry in the list.

Citation Detail — The Source template will appear with the cursor positioned on the Citation Detail portion of the template as shown in the following illustration.

Creating a New Source Citation

The cursor will be placed here

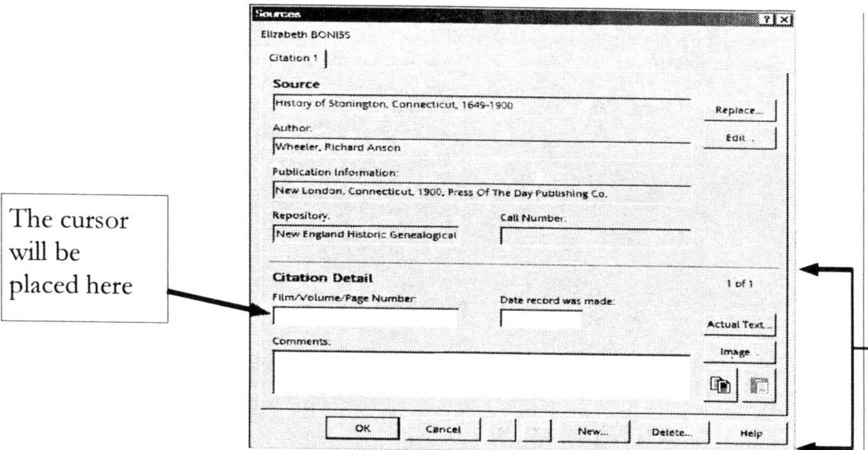

The Citation Detail portion of the Source template

Film/Volume/Page Number — Type the specific reference, such as the certificate number or page number, to the event you are documenting. Press *Tab* to move to the next field.

Date record was made — If available, enter the date the record was made, the date it was officially recorded, or the date it was microfilmed. Do not enter the date you are creating the citation entry.

See page 48 for more details about the *Date record was made* field.

Actual Text — Click the *Actual Text* button. The Citation Actual Text window will appear as shown below. Type the text exactly as it appears in the source and click on the *Save* button.

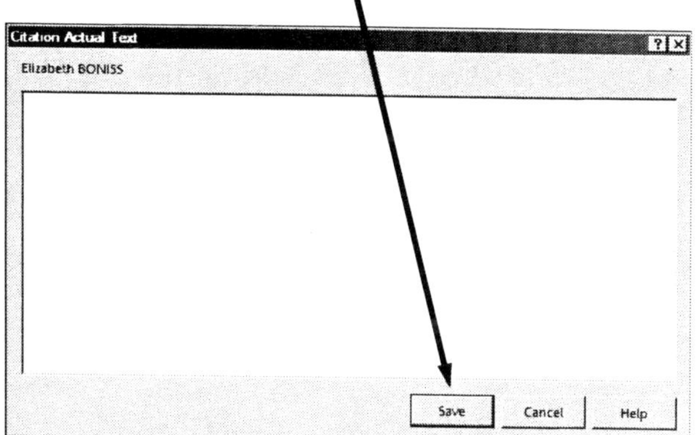

The Actual Text window for a citation

Comments — Enter any comments or explanations you might have concerning the citation. For example, describe how the date was calculated, assumptions drawn from the text, reliability of the details, or any conflicts with other sources.

Image button — If you wish to attach a photo, an audio file, or a video file documenting the source, click the *Image* button. The file must reside on your computer or on a storage disk. PAF only saves the path to

See Table A-6 for a list of acceptable file types for images.

Chapter Two: How to Create Sources

Creating a New Source Citation

The Attach Image window

the file, not the file itself. If the file is on a storage disk, the disk must be in the proper drive when using PAF, or an error message will occur when you try to display the image.

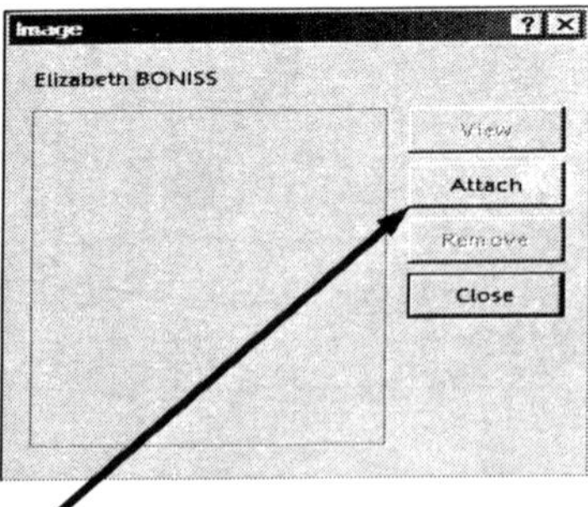

Click on the *Attach* button and use the Windows navigation browse function to locate the desired multimedia file. Click *OK* to attach the image to the event's documentation.

If you don't click on the *Select* button on the Select Source window, your entry will not be linked to the Individual.

Saving the Source Citation: Click the *OK* button on the Edit Source template to save the source description and the citation detail. Click Select to highlight the new Source entry and then click on the *Save* button on the Edit Individual window to save the record.

On the Edit Individual window, an asterisk (*) will appear next to the *s* or the *Individual Source* button showing that there is a source linked to that event. When there is more than one source attached to an event and you double-click one of the source selector buttons, the left and right arrows at the bottom of the Source template, or the Citation tabs at the top of the window will enable you to browse through the attached sources.

To scroll through multiple citation entries, click on the citation tabs or the left and right arrow buttons at the bottom of the window.

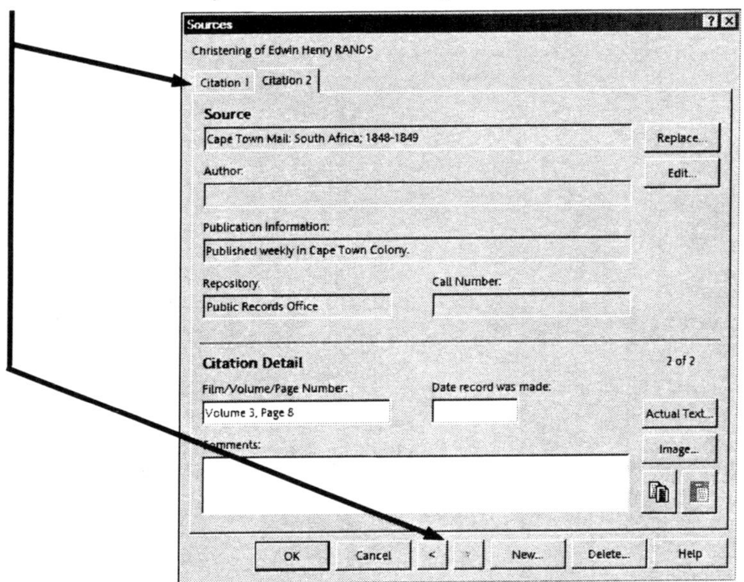

Since the source is now in the Source list, you can attach that source to another event for that same individual, or to an event for another individual. When you link a source to an event, make sure the source is not already entered on the Source list before you add a new entry. If it is already on your list, highlight it and click the *Select* button, or double-click on the entry.

How to Attach an Existing Source Citation

If the source entry you wish to use to document an event is already on the Source List, you can select it from the list and attach it to the event without retyping all the details. Once you have selected the desired source entry, the Source template will be displayed with the cursor positioned in the Citation Detail portion, ready for you to enter the unique information about the event.

The following steps explain the process in more detail.

Source selector buttons — From the Edit Individual window, double-click on the Source selector button (*s*) to the right of the event to which you wish to attach a source entry, or click on the *Individual Sources* button for non-event-related sources. The Select Source window will appear as shown below.

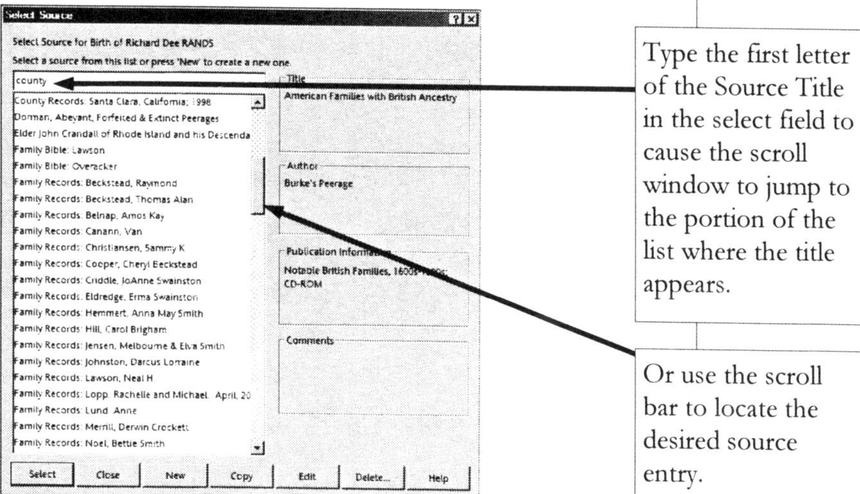

Search the list — Use the scroll bar to the right of the Source List to search the list for the source entry you wish to attach to your event. You may also enter the first letter of the Source Title in the Select field immediately above the Source List. As you enter a character, the list will automatically scroll to the portion of the window where the titles begin with the character you have typed.

Chapter Two: How to Create Sources

How to Attach an Existing Source Citation

Select button — When the Source entry you are looking for is in the Source List scroll window, you can now click on it to highlight it, and then click on the *Select* button to display the Source template. You may also double-click on the Source entry to display the Source template. As shown below, the cursor will be positioned in the first field of the Citation Detail portion of the window.

The Citation Detail portion of the Source template

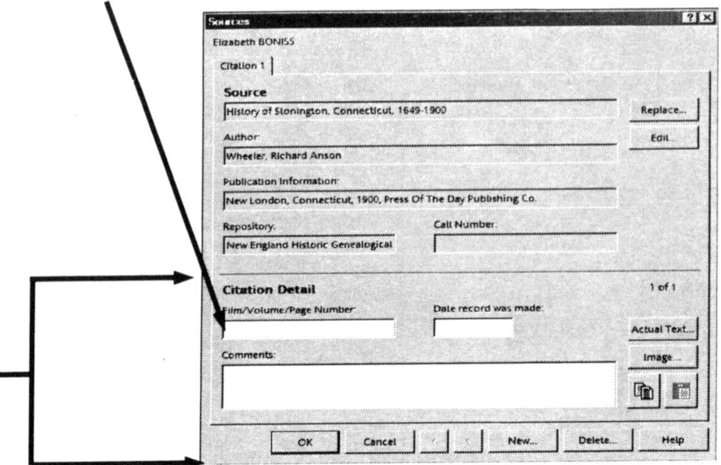

Film/Volume/Page Number — Type the specific reference, such as the certificate number or page number, to the event you are documenting. More details about the Citation Detail fields are given in the following Chapter. Press *Tab* to move to the subsequent field.

Date record was made — If the information is available, enter the date the record was made, the date it was officially recorded, or the date it was microfilmed. Do not enter the date you are creating the citation entry.

Actual Text — Click the *Actual Text* button. The Citation Actual Text window will appear as shown below. Type the text exactly as it appears in the source and click on the *Save* button.

Click on the *Save* button to save the actual text.

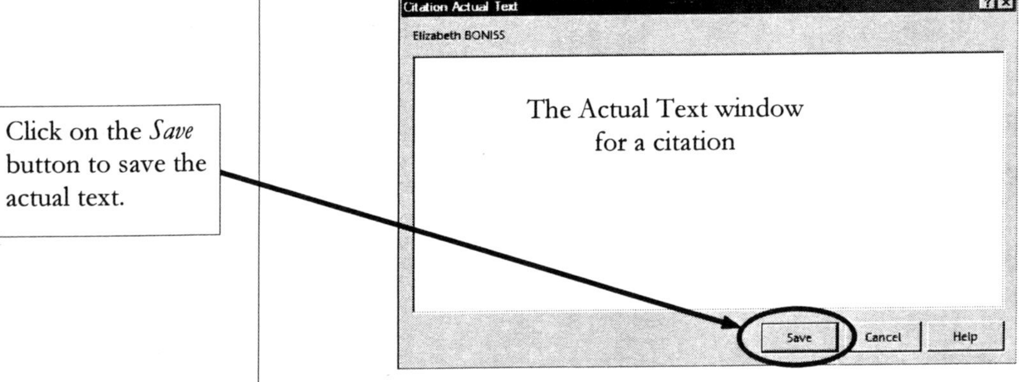

Comments — Enter any comments or explanations you might have concerning the citation. For example, describe how the date was calculated, assumptions drawn from the text, reliability of the details, or any conflicts with other sources.

Image button — If you wish to attach a photo of the source, click the *Image* button. The image can be a graphics file, an audio file, or a video file. The file must reside on your computer, or on a storage disk. Remember that PAF only saves the path to the file, not the file itself. If the file is on a storage disk, the disk must be in the proper drive when using PAF, or an error message will occur when you try to display the image.

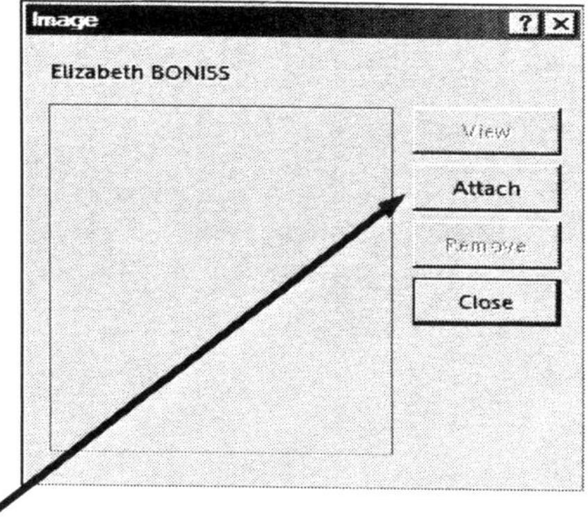

Click on the *Attach* button and use the Windows navigation browse function to locate the desired multimedia file. Click *OK* to attach the image to the event's documentation.

Saving the Source Citation — Click the *OK* button on the Edit Source template to save the source description and the citation detail. Click on the *Save* button on the Edit Individual window to save the record.

Another method of attaching an existing source to an event is to first select the source entry as described above, then memorize the citation by clicking on the *Memorize Citation* at the bottom right corner of the Source template. When you click on a Source selector button for an event, the Select Source window will now contain a *Use Memorized Citation* button in the lower right corner of the window.

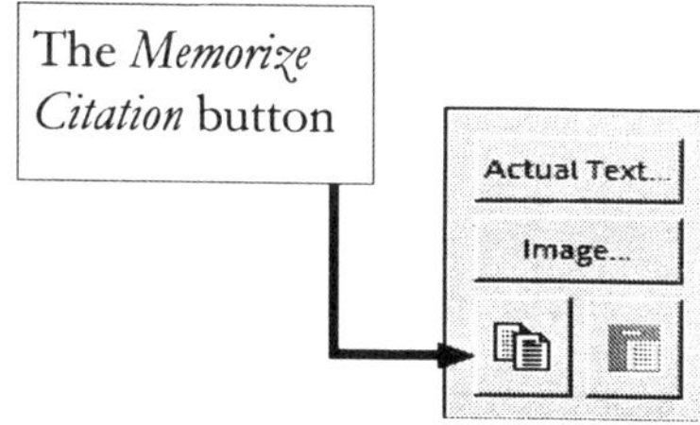

See Table A-6 for a list of acceptable file types for images.

This button will only appear on the Select Source window when a citation has been memorized. When you click on the *Use Memorized Citation* button, the entire memorized Source template will be displayed with the identical details as the Source and Citation you memorized.

You can now edit the Citation Detail to reflect the specific details that pertain to the event to which you are attaching the Source. The memorized source will not be affected by the changes you make unless you click the *Memorize Citation* button again.

Editing a Source Description — You can click on the *Edit* button to modify the Source description and the Repository. If you do edit the Source description, the changes will take effect on the Source description everywhere it is attached. Even if you change the Source Title, the new title will become the title of the Source entry everywhere it is attached. In PAF 3, if you change the Source description, a new Source citation is created.

A Difference in Source selector buttons between PAF 4 and 5 — In PAF 5, the *Individual Sources* button in the right margin of the Edit Individual window replaced the *s* button on the Title (suffix) line of PAF 4.

A difference between PAF 4 and PAF 5.

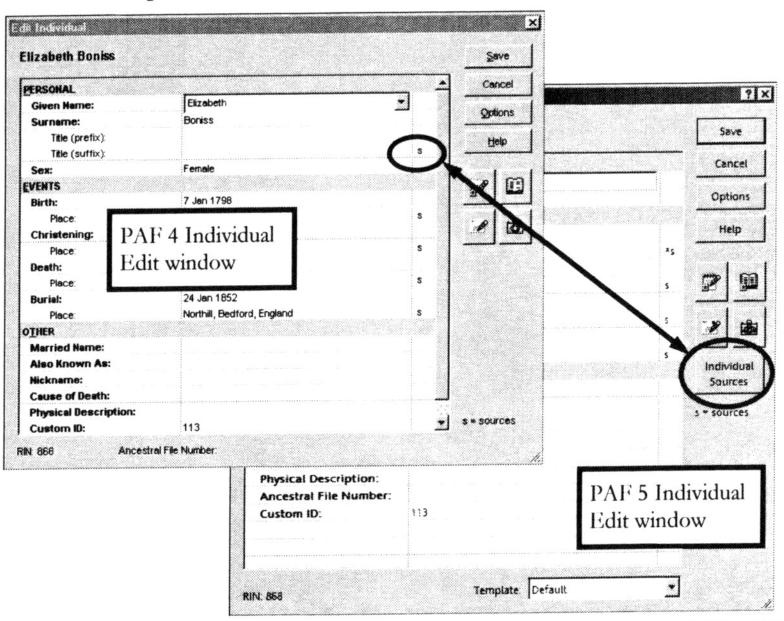

The (*s*) button on the suffix title line in PAF 4 and the *Individual Source* button in PAF 5 are intended for nonspecific source references. In some situations, the details about an individual do not contain a date for a birth or death. For example, a birth certificate may only indicate the names of the person's parents and not their birth dates or ages. Obituaries often mention survivors but leave out the details of their births. To cover such cases, PAF includes an additional place to put an individual's nonspecific source entries that do not contain direct evidence for dates and places of a birth, marriage, or death. This feature also may be used to document the source of information that is contained in the notes.

Likewise, the General Family Source selector that was located among the buttons on the right margin of the Edit Marriage window in PAF 4 has been moved to a similar location on the right margin in PAF 5 as shown below.

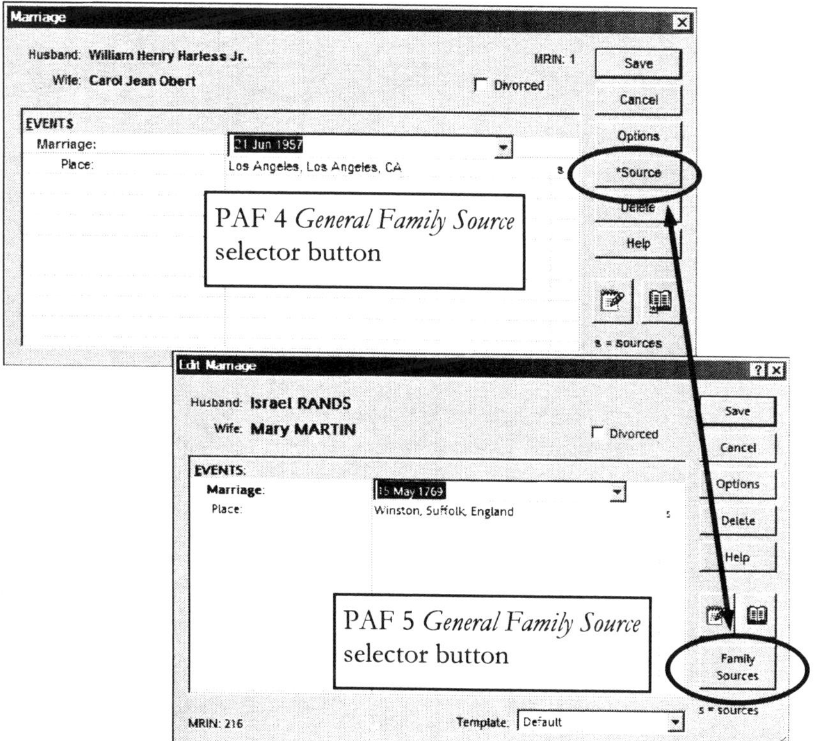

General family source citations should be used to document sources that confirm the marriage when there are no specific details that indicate the

General family source buttons are in different places in PAF 4 and PAF 5.

How to View Source Citations

Source entries may be viewed by clicking on the *View all sources* button, by pressing *Alt-R*, or by clicking on the *Sources* button from the *Options* menu of the Edit Individaul or Edit Marriage screens.

date and place of the marriage event. For example, if an obituary or a probate record refers to a spouse or to married surviving descendents, but gives no details of their marriage dates or places, use the general family source buttons to document the material.

A convenient way to view all the sources for an individual record or for a marriage record is to click on the *View all sources* button.

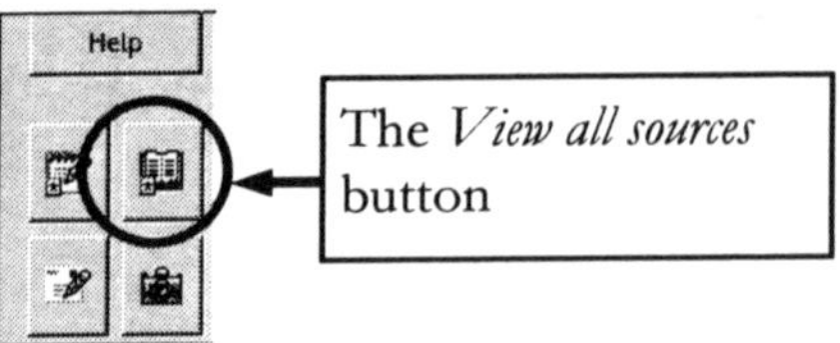

You may also press *Alt-R*, or click on the *Options* button on the right margin of the Edit Individual screen or the Edit Marriage screen and then click on the Sources button.

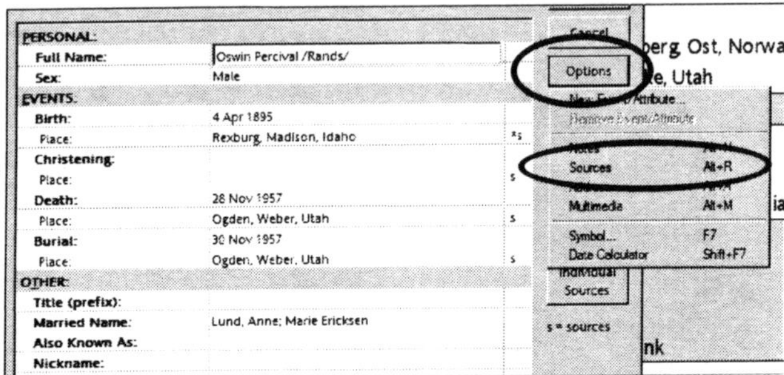

A View Sources screen will be displayed containing a formatted listing of all sources linked to the individual or marriage record.

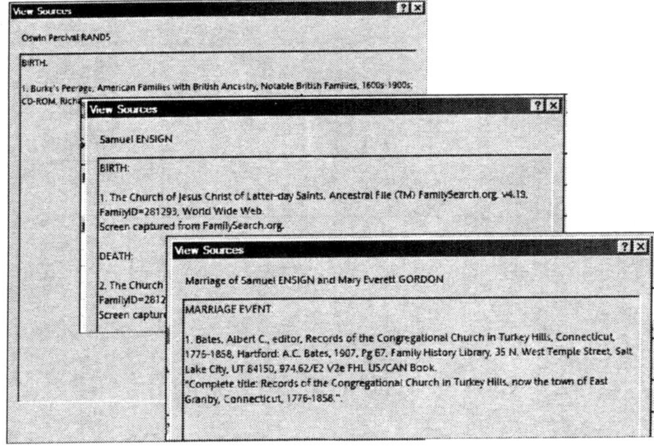

Chapter Three: PAF Source Template Guidelines

Source Templates

The Source template is a series of structured fields in which you describe the details about the source you are using to document an event. The PAF 5 source template shown below includes three sections: the overall Source Description; the Repository, or place where the document is located; and the Citation Detail, which contains the specific reference in

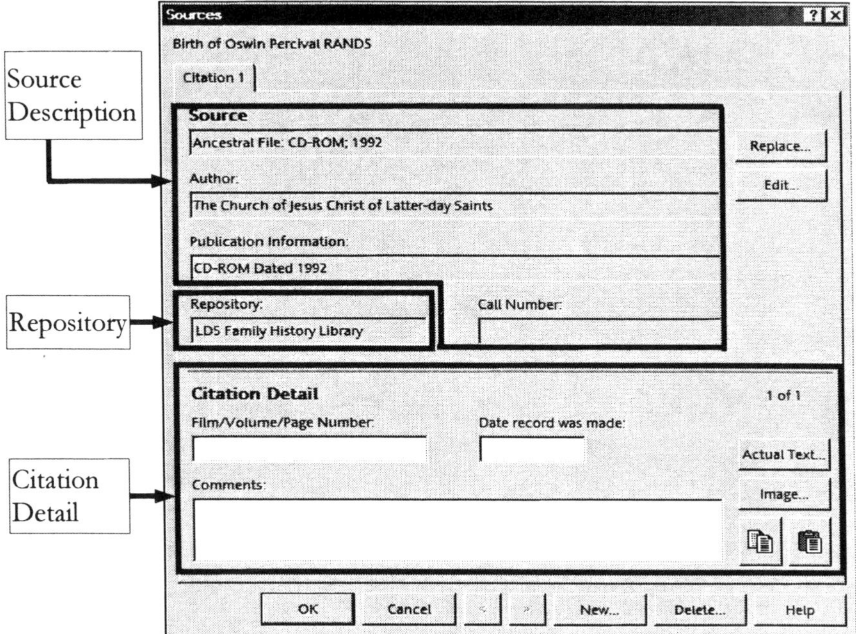

The Source Citation template

the source to the details of the event. (PAF 3 refers to these three sections as the Source Description, Repository, and Individual Reference.)

When a new source is being added, or an existing source is being replaced or modified, the Edit Source window is displayed.

Source Fields

The following section describes the guidelines for entering information in each of the fields. It is important to be clear, consistent, and thorough in entering the details about your source. The examples in Chapter Four will be helpful in understanding the recommendations.

Chapter Three: PAF Source Template Guidelines

Source Fields

The Edit Source window

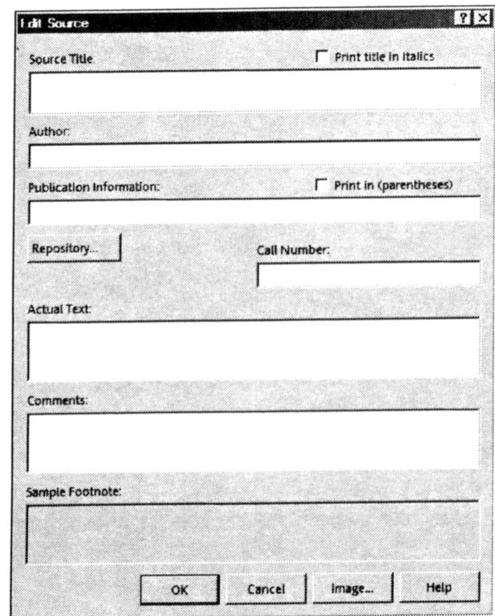

Use care when creating the Source Title.

The most important field in the Edit Source template is the source title, because that is what will appear in the Source List window, and is what you will need to select from the list when you want to link it to another event. Since the list is arranged alphabetically, the title should be composed in such a way that it will appear in the list where you would intuitively expect it to appear. As the list grows longer and longer, it is important to remember that what might be intuitive to you might not be intuitive to someone you share your database with. The objective of these guidelines is to promote a consistent method of naming sources so that you will be able to locate sources on the list quickly and will not duplicate entries for the same source, and so that your Source List will be consistent with those of others who share data with you. You may wish to use a combination of these methods, but you should be consistent for each format.

Three methods for composing a source title.

One method is to compose the title based on the type of document or the content of the document. For example, a census record would be described as follows:

One method is to compose the title based on the type of document or the content of the document.

Census: New York; 1860 U.S. Federal

Using this format will cause all census sources to appear together in order by date and place. Likewise, the IGI would be described as follows:

IGI: CD-ROM;1992 or IGI: FamilySearch.com; 2002

This format will cause the various versions of the IGI to be listed in order by release date. A collection of personal records containing many documents that are maintained together, such as a file cabinet belonging to a relative, would be described as follows:

Family Records: Midford, Sandra Lee

This has the advantage of reducing the source entry for many documents to a single entry. Each collection of family records will appear on the list in order by the surname of the owner. Published material should be listed by the actual title of the document according to normal publishing style. Using this method will cause all similar sources to appear in sequence in the Source List and will facilitate locating them when necessary. You will want to avoid being too specific, so that your Source List does not become so long and so complicated that you cannot easily locate entries.

A second method is to compose the title based on the geographical region covered by the source. For example, the census records would be listed by the geographical location covered by the census as follows:

New York: Census; 1860 U.S. Federal

Or you might have an entry such as this:

Ohio, Hancock County: Vital Records; 1914-1915

This method will cause all the sources for a location to appear in geographical sequence. Some researchers might find this method more useful when looking for source entries because they think of their family in terms of geographical areas. A combination of the two methods might be desirable to some, especially when some sources do not relate to a given geographical region.

A third method is to place the surname that the source refers to in the first position of the Source Title. This method might be helpful to those who organize their documentation by family names. For example:

Harrison, James: Family Bible; 1819

This can be awkward when documenting sources such as a census or other large database, especially when the source contains details about more than one surname.

Whatever format you choose should be comfortable for you, and, above all, should be consistent. The summary of the guidelines at the end of this chapter will also help clarify the recommendations. In the Edit Source window, use the following guidelines for each field:

Source Title — Enter a descriptive name or title of the source. For a published source, use the title of the source if it is a book or journal; use the title of the article if it is in a periodical. For unpublished sources, enter a descriptive title. See the above discussion of the significance of source titles and the ramifications of the different formats for a source title. Click on the *Print title in italics* box if the title is a published book. The title of an

A second method is to compose the title based on the geographical region covered by the source.

A third method is to place the surname that the source refers to in the first position of the Source Title.

Source titles can be printed in italics.

☐ Print title in italics

article in a periodical or newspaper usually is enclosed in parentheses.

Author — Enter the name of the author, editor, compiler, agency or institution that created the document. Enter individual names as surname, given name, and, when appropriate, a semicolon followed by the title, such as *editor*, *compiler*, or *translator*. If the source has two or three authors, list the names of the authors. If there are more than three, write *et al.* after the third name.

Publication Information can be printed in parentheses for footnotes.

Print in (parentheses)

Publication Information — For published materials, the place of publication is followed by a colon, the name of the publisher, and the date of publication. When the source entry is going to be printed as a footnote in a book, the publication information should be enclosed in parentheses. Click on the *Print in (parentheses)* box to cause the information to print in footnote form.

A trick for causing titles of periodicals to be italicized on printed reports.

If the source is an article from a periodical, enter the name of the periodical. Since it is customary to print the title of a periodical in italics, and since there is not a check box to print this field in italics, you will need to use a clever technique to "trick" PAF into printing the name of the periodical in italics on printed reports. If you enclose the title of the periodical between codes as follows: <I>title of periodical</I>, it will be printed in italics. A volume and date should be included here if the article is complete in one issue. For example:

<I>The New York Times</I>, 1901-1905

If the source material is privately published, enter the appropriate facts. If it is unpublished information, enter the form of the record, such as a certificate, microfilm, photocopy, CD-ROM, funeral program, copy of an e-mail, downloaded file from a Web site, birth announcement, or wedding invitation.

Avoid violating the privacy of others. Get permission before including a person's address.

Repository — List the name and address of the library, archive, government agency, or a person's home where the records can be found. If the records are in your personal library, name yourself as the repository. If they are in another person's possession, give the name but do not record more than a city for the address without getting permission from the person.

If the record was borrowed from the Family History Library, give the name and address of the Family History Library in Salt Lake City, even if the microfilm or microfiche was read in a Family History Center in another city. If the source was searched in a Family History Center but was not borrowed from the Family History Library, enter the name and address of the Family History Center where you read the records as the repository.

See Table A-8 for frequently used repository addresses.

Call Number — Enter the library call number, the film number, or similar record identification number of the source as a whole If the source is contained on more than one microfilm, enter the range of the film numbers. This must be the number used by the specified repository. If the record is in your possession, you can enter your own identification number or code.

Actual Text (Not available in PAF 3) — Enter any text from the source that is general enough to apply to all possible entries from that source. For example, part of the introduction in a book, or an excerpt from the acknowledgements about the authenticity of the data, or how it was collected. Only enter the text that you want to be included in every use of the source.

Comments — This is a good place to enter any problems with the source. Examples are as follows:

- "Microfilm is hard to read."
- "Document written in old-style handwriting."
- "Index of the census with incomplete information."
- "Images of original records."
- "Transcript of original records."

After you have entered the source information in the Edit Source window, click *OK* to return to the Source List. Highlight the entry you have just created and click on the *Select* button. Now you can enter the specific citation details in the Source template using the following guidelines.

Citation Detail

The Citation Detail contains the specific details relating to the event you are documenting.

Film/Volume/Page Number — Enter the volume number, page number, the particular film number, item number, or frame number, if appropriate. Include a certificate number or record number, if appropriate. If the source is a Web page, enter the URL address.

Date record was made — This is the date the data was entered in the original record or the date the record was recorded by a government agency. Do not enter the date you enter it into your database. This could be the date the birth or death certificate was recorded or perhaps the date the census was taken.

Comments — This field can be used to discuss possible contradictions with other data, how calculated or estimated dates were determined, or references to the Notes screen for more complete discussion of a problem.

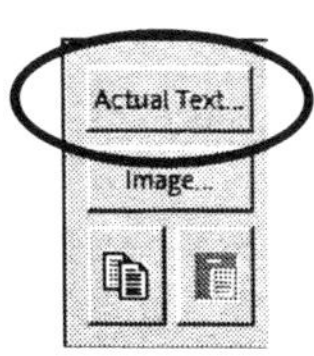

Actual Text — To enter actual text from the source as part of the citation detail, click on the *Actual Text* button. In the Actual Text window,

Chapter Three: PAF Source Template Guidelines

Citation Detail

PAF 5 automatically inserts quote marks in the Actual Text field.
In PAF 4 you must insert them manually.

enter a transcription of that portion of the text that refers to the event being documented. When the actual text is long, use only the part of it that applies to the event being documented. Enclosing a textual transcription within quotation marks helps to assure the reader that the quotation is accurate. However, sometimes using quotation marks is unnecessary, such as when the information is taken from the columns of a census record or a parish record. Specifying the column headings within square brackets will clarify the entry. For example:

> "Harriot Phillips [born] 21 Nov 1832 [parents] Edward and Diana Phillips [baptized] 23 Nov 1832 [by] John Evans [Vicar]"

The following are available in PAF 4 and 5, but not in PAF 3.

Image — A scanned image of a certificate or of a document can be included, but remember that it will not be printed on reports. The words in an image are not searchable using Focus/Filter, and the image will not be included in a GEDCOM file or a backup file. The important text in the image should be included in the Actual Text field. For a list of acceptable multimedia file formats, see Table A-6 in the Appendix.

Sample Footnote — This field shows how the footnote will appear in the printed reports. You cannot edit this field directly. You must edit the individual fields in the template to change the footnote format. In PAF 4 this field does not display a title that you specify to be printed in italics, but will indicate the words that will be printed in italics by a code before and after those words. PAF 5 will display the title in an italic font. The sample footnote will give you the opportunity to make changes in your source description if you desire to do so.

In the footnote sample for PAF 4, italics will be shown as follows:
<I>this text is in italics</I>

In the footnote sample for PAF 5, a title will be displayed in an italic font.

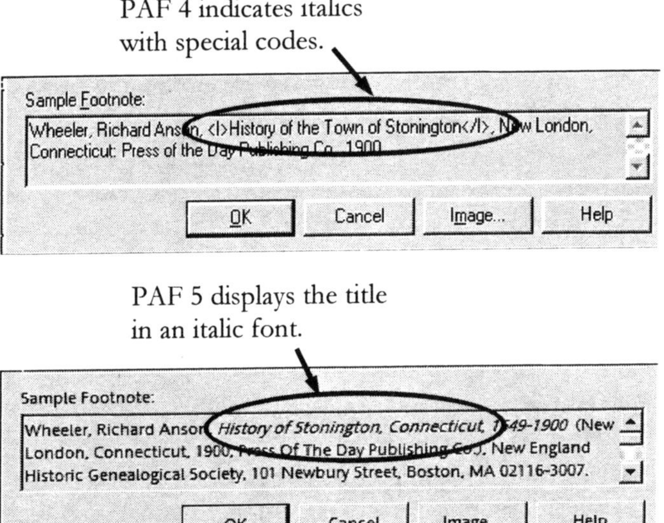

Additional Considerations for Using the PAF Source System

Attaching Source Descriptions — Source citations can be attached to events on the Edit Individual window, including the birth, christening, death, burial; and attached to the individual as a general information source. Every event where there is an *s* to the right of the field can have a source citation attached to it. General information sources about the person can be attached in the personal section by clicking on the *s* after the Title (suffix) field in PAF 4, or by clicking on the *Individual Sources* button in PAF 5. Sources for marriage information should be attached to events on the Marriage screen. You can also attach sources to Other Events. The Other Events window is accessed by clicking on the *Options* button on the Edit Individual window and choosing *New Event/Attribute.*

Source Titles — As discussed in the guidelines (pages 25-30), the title of your source determines how it will appear and where in the sequence it will appear in the Source List. The several options and the ramifications of each have been outlined. Essentially, you organize your Source List by the way you enter the titles. It is best to experiment with a few sources. You can always edit the source and change the title if you don't like the way your list is shaping up. In PAF 4 and 5, changing the title in the Edit mode changes the source wherever it is attached.

Actual Text Fields in Source Description and Citation Detail — Both the Source Description and the Citation Detail templates contain an Actual Text field. The text you want to appear every time you cite the source should be entered in the Actual Text field of the source description. It will then appear each time you cite that source. Text that only applies to a particular event should be entered in the Citation Detail Actual Text field, so that it only appears on records for the event of that specific individual.

Examples of actual text in a source description include the subtitle of a book, the introduction to a church parish record, a one-page text that applies to several individuals, or other text that should accompany the source each time it is cited. Remember when using PAF 4 to place quote marks around exact text. PAF 5 will insert them automatically.

Examples of actual text in a citation detail include transcriptions of wills, letters, journal entries, biographies, information in a census record, or other document. Text in the citation detail also can summarize the information on birth, marriage, death, or other types of certificates. Even if you attach a scanned image of the document, you should enter the actual text so that you can search on words in the text using the Focus/Filter feature, and so the actual text will also be printed on reports and in books.

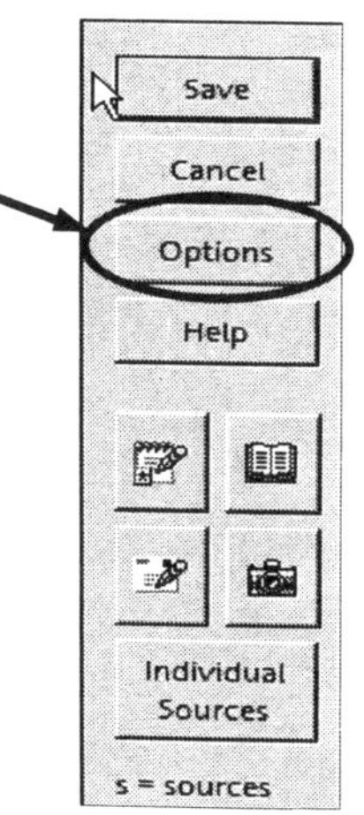

In PAF 3, changing the title in the Edit mode creates a new source entry.

Chapter Three: PAF Source Template Guidelines

Additional Considerations

When you use the Focus/Filter feature, the Source Text option on the Possible Fields list applies only to the Actual Text field in the source description. To find certain words in the Citation Actual Text field, on the Possible Fields list, choose *Sources, All.*

If desired, you can make a notation in the Citation Detail Actual Text field that the full text of the document can be found in the notes section with the appropriate tag noted.

Comments Fields in Source Description and Citation Detail — Both the Source Description template and the Citation Detail template contain a Comments field. The Comments field in the Source Description template will appear every time you cite that source. It may be used for such notations as the condition of the document, directions to the actual repository, location of copies of the source, instructions for using a particularly difficult source, the name of software required to access a source in digital format, and any other comments that would be helpful to someone using the source. Other helpful comments could include the number of pages in the source and whether or not a book is indexed.

Comments in the Citation Detail could include conclusions drawn from the information found in the source, analyses of the data such as date calculations and possible relationships, or notes concerning potential areas for future research or conflicts in information to be resolved.

Be sure to document a source within a source.

Sometimes the source you are referencing cites another source. An example would be a biography that refers to a family Bible record. Your source might even quote verbatim from another source and give enough information that someone could find that other source. We refer to this situation as *having a source within a source.* Since you have not actually seen the source referred to, you cannot use it as a source, but you should make a reference to it in the Comments field. In the example just given, you might note in the Comments field of the Citation Detail, "References Smith Family Bible, copy in possession of Mrs. John Smith, Hometown, USA."

Be careful to avoid violating the privacy of others.

Privacy considerations in sources — Since you might share your data with others, submit it to a database that can be viewed by the public, or post it on the Internet, privacy is an important consideration in both the Repository and the Comments fields. When listing an individual as a Repository, be sure to get permission from the person before including his or her name and address in your database. When making comments, be aware that others might read them, and be respectful of personal feelings and their right to privacy. Be especially tactful in family matters such as adoption, illegitimacy, divorce, and other events or happenings that could be embarrassing or hurtful to others if made public.

Replacing Citations — If a Citation Detail should be attached to a different source, click on the *Replace* button on the Source screen. A warning appears that you are about to replace the source that the citation refers to. If you continue and choose another source from the Source list, or create a new source, the citation will be removed from the original source and attached to the second source. This procedure could be handy to correct a mistake made while entering a source.

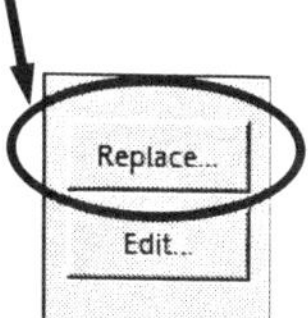

Adding Multiple Sources — Any number of sources can be attached to any life event, custom event, or attribute, or to the individual in general. Click on the *New* button on the Source screen and create the additional source. When there is more than one source, the left and right arrows at the bottom of the screen will be highlighted. A Citation tab will appear at the top of the screen for each source, allowing you to view each source in turn by clicking on the appropriate arrow or tab.

Multiple citation tabs

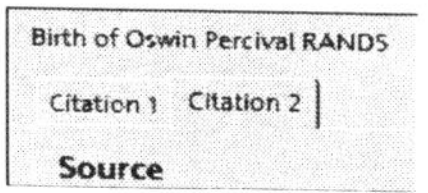

Copying a Source Entry — Occasionally you will encounter the need to add a new source citation that is very similar to one already in your list. You can easily duplicate the existing entry and then edit the copy to make a new entry. From the Source List window, select the entry you wish to copy and click on the *Copy* button at the bottom of the window. Then click on the *Edit* button to complete the new entry.

To make a duplicate copy of a Source citation for an event from the Edit Source template, or to copy it to another event, click on the *Memorize Citation* button on the Edit Source window. The information in all the fields will be saved to the Windows clipboard.

The *Memorize Citation* button

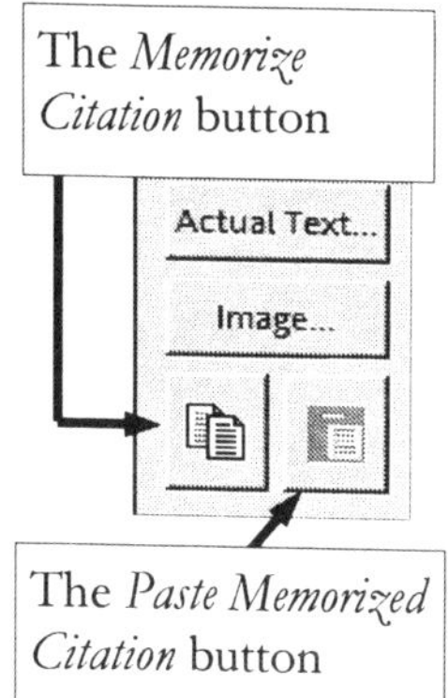

The *Paste Memorized Citation* button

To add a duplicate copy of the citation to the event, click on the *Paste Memorized Citation* button. The new citation will be displayed so that you can edit as needed to make it a unique source citation. If you wish to use this Source citation for another event, either for the same individual, or another individual, go to the target Source screen and click on the *Use Memorized Citation* button. The information in all the fields will be attached to the new event.

The usual Windows commands for cutting, copying and pasting also apply in each individual field of the Source Description and Citation Detail screens. Highlight the text to be copied, press *Ctrl-C* to copy it, open the target source citation, and, with your cursor in the appropriate field, press *Ctrl-V* to paste the text.

Removing a Source from the Source List — If you no longer need a source, or discover it is incorrect, you can completely delete it from your database. You can remove it either from the full Source List or from an individual record to which the source is attached. From the Individual Edit screen, double click the ***s*** referencing the source to be deleted, then click on

New to display the Source List. Locate the source entry you wish to delete and click on it once to select and highlight it. Click on the *Delete* button, and then click *Yes* when prompted to complete the deletion.

To delete a source directly from the Source List, pull down the *Edit* menu and select Source List. Highlight the source to be deleted and click on the *Delete* button. When prompted, click on *Yes* to complete the process. It is important to realize that a deleted source will be removed from every place it is referenced, so be sure you want to completely remove the source from your database before performing a delete procedure.

Removing a Source from an Individual — If you want to remove a source from a particular record, but keep it in your database, double click the ***s*** on the Edit Individual or Edit Marriage screen that references the source you wish to remove. If there is more than one source attached to the record, click the **>** button until the source you want to remove is displayed. Click *Delete*, and, when prompted, click *Yes* to complete the process. The source will be removed from that individual or marriage record but will remain in the Source List.

Removing a Repository — To remove a repository from a source, open the Edit Source window of the source citation from which you want to remove the repository. You can either select *Source List* on the *Edit* menu and click on the source that contains the repository you wish to remove. Or you can go to the Edit Source window by clicking on a Source Selector button for an event where the desired source citation is attached. Click *Edit*, then *Repository*. In the list of repositories, highlight <<*no repository*>> and click *Select*.

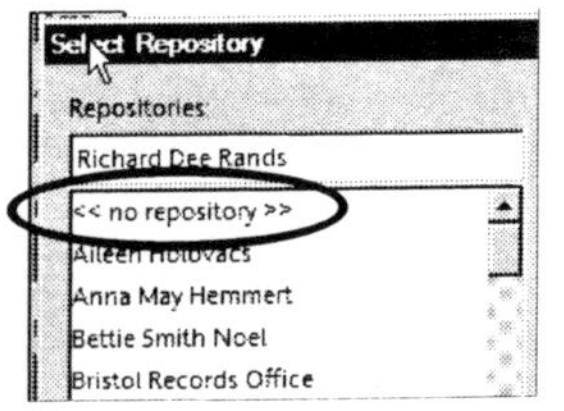

The source will remain on the source list, but with no repository specified. If desired, you can select or add another repository. This procedure might be necessary if the repository is no longer in existence, or if you find the same source in a more convenient location.

Appearance of Printed Sources in Books created by PAF— Sources are printed at the end of the book when printing either an ancestry (Ahnentafel) book or a descendancy (Modified register) book. Superscripted numbers in the text of the book reference each source and run consecutively throughout the book. Another option is to print the sources at the end of each chapter. Again, superscripted numbers in the text of the chapter refer to the sources listed at the end of the chapter, and the numbers begin again with *1* in each chapter.

Example of a superscript in the text of an ancestry book:

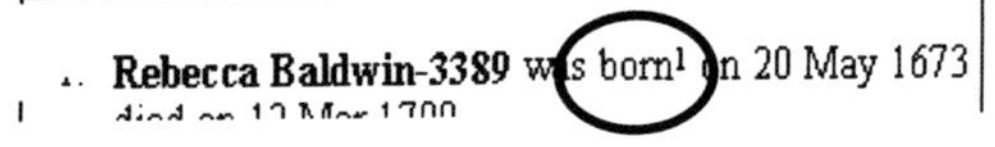

Additional Considerations

Appearance of Footnotes — Another consideration in entering sources is the appearance of the source in the footnotes on various print-outs such as family group sheets, reports, and books. You can view the formation of the footnote at the bottom of the screen as you enter the information in the source template. If it looks too long, too involved, or is in an improper format, changes can be made in either the source or the citation templates by using the Edit function.

Viewing Sources — Sources can be viewed in any of several ways. From the Edit Individual screen, click on any *s* with an asterisk next to it (**s*) to view the source or sources for that particular event. To view all the sources for an individual, press *Alt-R* on the Edit Individual screen or click on the Source icon that is depicted by a figure of an open book. From the Notes screen, click on the *Sources* button at the bottom of the screen. An asterisk added to this button means sources are attached to this individual record.

From the Notes screen, if there are no sources attached to the individual, the *Sources* button is dimmed.

Factors to Consider When Printing — Printing the Actual Text and Comments fields is optional when printing family group sheets and various other reports and books. Consider carefully what you want included on the printout, since the complete actual text of many sources could consume a lot of paper and not be necessary.

When printing Family Group Records, two choices are worth noting. You can specify Parents Only to reduce the amount of printing, you can specify that only the Titles of Source entries be printed, or you can omit the sources' Actual Text and Comments. These options are available on the Print Options window as shown below. The Actual Text is not repeated each time a Source description is printed on Family Group Records.

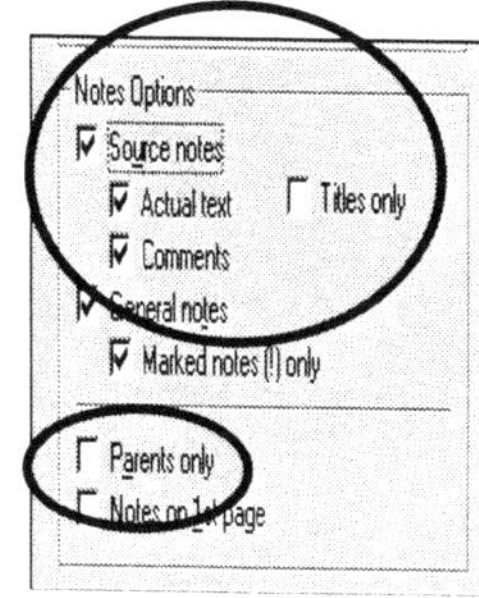

Note: As part of the printing process in PAF, you are allowed to preview any printout to make sure it will print correctly. Experiment by selecting the various printing options and clicking the *Preview* button to see how the printout will appear. You can zoom two levels in to enlarge the screen and see exactly what text is being included in the various printing options, and make any desired changes before you actually print or save to a file.

Printing the Source List — Located on the *List* tab of the Print menu is an option to print all Sources, which will generate an alphabetical list of sources including the title, author, publication information, repository, call number, and comments. Such a list can help you determine if you already have a source listed and if you have the Source List organized in the most helpful manner for your purposes.

Printing a List of Citations Referencing a Particular Source — Also on the *List* tab of the Print menu is an option to locate all the citations attached to a particular source. When you check this box and click either the *Print* button or the *Preview* button, you are brought to the Source List. Highlight a source and click the *Select* button at the bottom of the screen. PAF then searches through all the citations and locates the ones attached to the highlighted source. The report shows the name of the source; any text and comments; the repository; and a listing of individuals with RIN, type of event, and Film/Volume/Page number entry for each citation. A possible use for this report would be for you to pull up one of the citations to the screen, use the *Memorize Citation* button, and paste it in a new citation to avoid duplicate typing of the data.

Table A-6 in the appendix lists the multimedia file formats you can use.

Adding Multimedia to Sources (not available in PAF 3) — You can attach a scanned image, an audio file, or a video file to either a source or a citation by clicking on the *Image* button, choosing *Attach*, and entering the information regarding the type of multimedia and the path to the file. Possibilities for scanned images include documents, certificates, pages from a book or journal, maps, photographs, or photocopies from microfilms or microfiches. Sound files could include clips from taped interviews or a recording of someone speaking into a computer microphone. Video clips could be from family reunions or videotaped interviews. See Table A-6 in the Appendix for a list of acceptable multimedia file formats.

Whatever the source may be, there is a way in PAF to record the details completely and preserve it for future reference by yourself and other researchers.

Remember to backup your multimedia files separately. They are not saved during a normal PAF back up.

Remember that PAF records only the paths to the multimedia files, not the files themselves. When you backup your database, or create a GEDCOM file, the multimedia files are not included, only the paths to those files. The recipient of the GEDCOM file must also have access to those same multimedia files with the identical path (including both drive and name of the file) or an error message will occur when the *Image* button is clicked.

If the recipient of the GEDCOM file stores the multimedia files on a drive lettered differently than the drive where the GEDCOM file originated, the multimedia path name can be changed by selecting *Tools, Global Search and Replace*, and, on the pull-down menu, choosing *Multimedia File Names.* The recipient can then change the link to the correct path so that the multimedia files can be viewed when the GEDCOM file has been imported into a PAF database. The multimedia files will need to be sent separately on storage media, or sent as an e-mail attachment.

Publishing Your Data — If you plan to publish your data in hard copy, in digital format, or on the Web, the source documentation that you include will make the difference between your data being just a collection of names and being a meaningful genealogical record.

Additional Considerations

Using the Other Events Templates — On the Edit Individual screen, click on the *Options* button and choose *New Event/Attribute.* A list of event labels will appear as shown below.

The Select Event window

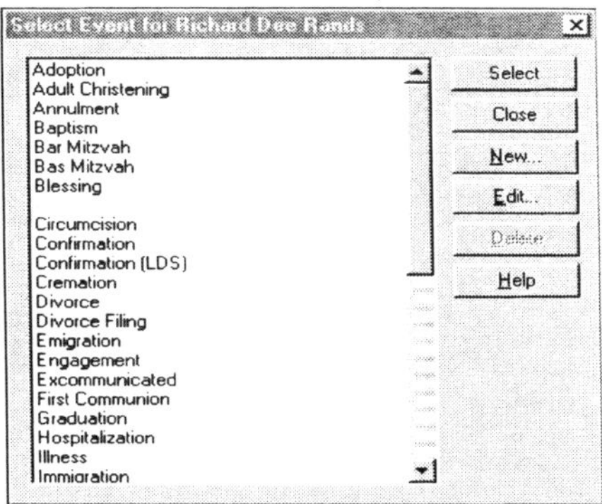

This allows you to choose one of the preset labels or to create a new event of your choice.

Selecting one of the labels will place that event on the Edit Individual screen by creating a new section labeled Other Events. You can now enter a date and place for that event and attach a source. Some of the labels, such as Hospitalization, Residence, Mission, and Illness contain other fields, such as beginning and ending dates and a description. All of the labels allow you to specify that the information is confidential.

Table 3-1: Other Events Available for Documentation

Other Event labels

Adoption	Divorce	Miscarriage
Adult Christening	Divorce Filing	Mission
Annulment	Emigration	Move
Baptism	Engagement	Naming
Bar Mitzvah	Excommunicated	Naturalization
Bas Mitzvah	First Communion	Occupation
Birth	Graduation	Ordinance
Blessing	Hospitalization	Ordination
Burial	Illness	Probate
Census	Immigration	Religion
Christening	Marriage Contract	Residence
Circumcision	Marriage License	Retirement
Confirmation	Marriage Notice	Separation
Cremation	Marriage Settlement	Will
Death	Military Service	

Confusion may arise due to the fact that many of the Other Event labels are duplicates of the suggested Notes tags. The decision to enter your information as an Other Event or a Note will be influenced by the following factors:

- **Printing Options —** If you choose to print the Other Events fields on a Family Group Sheet, they appear between the Christening field and the Death field. If you have many Other Events, the person's record will extend for many lines.

  You cannot choose to print only some of the Other Events — you get all or none, unless you mark them as Confidential. Do not print confidential notes or events.

  When printing an Individual Summary, you do not have an option to print only non-confidential Other Events. Therefore, you should use care when adding event labels for confidential events.

  The appearance of source entries in books is affected by whether information is entered in Other Events or in the Notes screen. If you choose to print the Other Events data, they are incorporated in text format in the person's biography. You have the option of embedding the Notes so that they print in list format after the biography, or of printing them as an appendix at the end of each chapter.

  Try the various printing options and preview the print image to see which option you prefer.

- **Sources for Other Events —** The sources for Other Events go into the master Source List. If you do not want that list to be excessively long, it will be better to add the Other Event information as notes.

- **Relevance of the Information —** Since you can create any number of custom Other Event labels, caution should be used not to fill up the database with items that would be better placed in a scrapbook about the individual, such as contest prizes, travel, hobbies, and athletic achievements. While the use of Notes and Other Events entails personal preferences, a study of the section on the differences between Notes and Sources can help you decide what to include in your database and where to place the information.

- **Entry Format —** Because Other Events are entered into a template, the format is more structured; therefore, Focus/Filter searches will be more precise than an entry in the Notes screen, which can be less structured.

Defining Custom Events — If the event tag you want is not on the list, you can create your own Custom Event by clicking on the *New* button of the Select Event window. The Define Custom Event window will appear as shown below.

Window for creating custom event labels

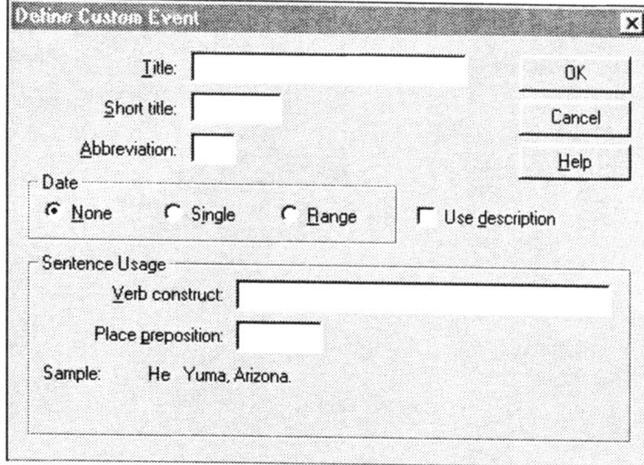

- **Titles** — Enter a title that will become the full name of the event that will appear on the Select Other Event window. Give the event a short title that will be used when printing reports, and a two-letter abbreviation for use when printing very compact reports.
- **Date** — Choose the date format from among the following: no date at all, a single date, or a range of time.
- **Use Description** — Click on the *Use Description* box if you want the event description to be inserted in the sentence describing the event when you print a book.
- **Sentence Usage** — The Verb Construct and Place Preposition fields are used to compose a grammatical sentence for the event when printing in a book. For example, suppose the custom event is "knighted." You would enter into the Verb Construct field, "was knighted" and you would enter the preposition "in" in the Place Preposition. Assuming you specified a single date for the event, the sentence would appear as follows:

  He was knighted 3 Mar 1689 in Surrey, England.

Since the Sentence Usage structure is based on English sentence syntax, you should expect to see changes in this screen in future releases to accommodate other languages.

Merging Sources and Repositories

Merging Sources and Repositories — PAF will automatically merge sources and repositories that are word-for-word identical. It will not merge sources or repositories that differ by even one character. PAF will not

To merge sources and repositories, click on the *Tools* menu. Then select *Merge Duplicate Sources and Citations.*

merge "California: Birth Certificate" and "Birth Certificate: California," even though they are essentially the same source. The merge is automatic, and PAF will tell you only how many sources were merged and how many repositories were merged, as shown in the window below. It will not identify which ones were merged. This feature is handy if you have imported a GEDCOM file from someone else's database, since each source and repository in the GEDCOM file will be added separately to your source and repository lists, and many of them may be duplications.

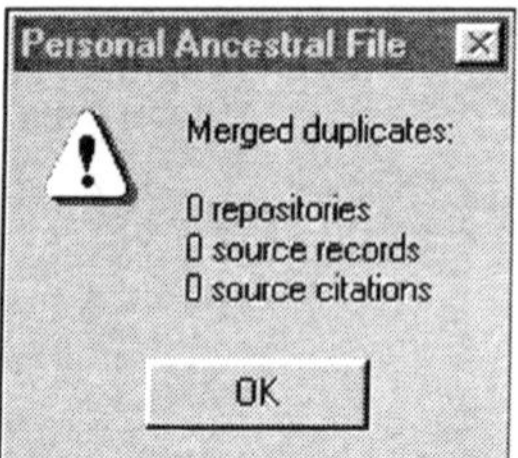

If you delete duplicate sources or repositories, the citations attached to them will be lost. It is necessary to merge duplicate sources for citations to remain and to be attached to a source. If duplicate sources do not automatically merge, you must edit them until they are exactly the same.

Summary of Guidelines for Source Citations

Source Titles

Before entering sources haphazardly, consider the powerful tools that are now available for copying and editing sources, and plan accordingly:

- A *Source Description* is entered once, and becomes part of an *alphabetized Source List.* It is then available to be used again and again for different individual records and different events, without having to be retyped.
- The wording of the title should be carefully considered, because *how it is worded* determines how it shows up on the list — the *first word* is key to grouping related information, such as by record type, place name, or by family name, thus making it easier to find.
- Changing any field in the Source Description, or the Repository, including the Source Title, will automatically be reflected everywhere that source is attached. There is an exception for PAF 3.
- In PAF 3, when the Title in the Source Description is changed in any way, it creates a new Source entry. To correct the Title without creating a new source, the only way is to create a new source and then merge them using the Match/Merge feature.

The following are basic rules for entering Source Titles:

- For a *published book or article, use the title* on the title page.
- Use exact titles; titles will be sorted in alphabetical order throughout the Source List. An exact title can always be identified without question by researchers.
- Enter the entire title and click the *Print Title in Italics* box. If the title includes multiple names, include up to three authors, followed by *et al.* For example:

  Smith, Jones and Miller Families,The – Early American Pioneers
  A Hundred Travelers In Veracruz, Volume 8, 1896-1925

- Decide which of the three recommended formats to use that will best identify the source.
- The entry in the title field should be complete enough to recognize it in a list of sources. (For example, *Death Certificate 1* and *Death Certificate 2* or *Letter* are not specific enough to identify the source.) It should be general enough to use for more than one source entry.

What you enter as a Source Title will determine where it is listed in the Source List.

Chapter Three: PAF Source Template Guidelines

Summary of Guidelines for Source Citations

- If the range of years of events covered by the source is available, include it with the title. Enclose the range of dates in parentheses to indicate that the year range was not included as part of the title name.

  Robert Fletcher and His Descendants (1600-1883)

- *A published database* is capitalized but not italicized:

  Ancestral File or Pedigree Resource File

See pages 42-43 to print the name of a periodical in italics.

- The title of an *article in a periodical or newspaper* should be enclosed in quotation marks. (Note: The name of a *periodical or newspaper* is entered in the Publication Information field in italics.)
- Sometimes a source will actually be a quote or extraction from another source. For example: A book lists a parish register as a reference. When a source (in this case, a book) is a secondary source that contains references to primary sources or records, use the title of the book as your source title. Record all the information about the parish register in Actual Text and Comments of the Citation Detail section.
- For an *unpublished work*, enter a descriptive title that clearly and uniquely identifies the material.
- Where there is a possibility of multiple source citations, it is convenient to select a title that is general enough to be used in many different applications, with the specific source described in the Citation Detail.

Three recommended methods for composing Source Titles

The same source can be entered in several ways — by record type, by place, or by surname.

When listed by *record type*, follow these recommendations:

- Use source titles that reflect the name of a collection of like items that contain details of many events that will result in the source reference being used many times in your documentation. These are examples:

  Census: Pennsylvania; 1850 U.S. Federal

  Vital Records: California; 1930-1935

  Probate Records: California; 1895-1899

  Parish Records: Raude Parish, Hannover, Prussia; 1770-1771

  Family Records: Smith, Nathanial Wilson

  Family Bible: Lunde, George

When listed by *place:*

- Since sources will be grouped by place name, all sources for the same geographical area will be together. The sequence for place is greater to lesser: country, state, county, city.

    Prussia, Hannover, Raude Parish: Baptism Record

- For the United States, start with state.
- Some may prefer the reverse order, but this could result in places with different names in the same area being listed separately:

    Raude Parish, Hannover, Prussia: Baptism Record

- Sometimes the full place name is not necessary:

    Pennsylvania: Census, 1850 U.S. Federal
    California: Vital Records Office

- Avoid abbreviations if possible. Some exceptions:

    U.S., as in U.S. Federal Census
    Co., when the record is at the county level.

When listed by *surname:*

- It is not recommended to list each certificate under the unique name of the person. This will result in a very long source list. These and other records should be entered under the more generic "place" or "type," with the specifics recorded in the Source Citations.
- At times, the name is the best way to begin a title. Be sure to record the surname first. If it would be helpful, add the year of birth in parentheses at the end of the name. When a number of generations have the same given name, the year of birth would help distinguish them. Also, the span of years for the journal or correspondence or interviews could be added:

    Smith, Virginia (1902): journal (1920-1945)

- Instead of listing each letter or interview, group them by the author's name; then you can detail each item in a separate Source Citation.

    Brady, Ann: Letters (or Correspondence)
    Jones, Janice (1915): Interview

- A record or artifact referring to one individual can be recorded under the name:

    Montgomery, Nelson (1902): engraved silver baby cup
    Wong, May Ling (1967): cremation remains
    Yarbrough, Carl (1945): commemorative plaque

You may wish to use a combination of the three different formats.

Chapter Three: PAF Source Template Guidelines

Summary of Guidelines for Source Citations

Another option is a *combination of surname and place or type.*

- List the family name or name of an individual at the *beginning* of a source title – either a book or other published source, or geographical listing, or event.
- Since all the records of one individual or family are grouped together, they are easy to find and reuse. However, this does lead to longer source titles. Also, only one surname begins the title, and the record could contain references to many other surnames. In this case it would be difficult to know where to look for records when they are listed under a different surname.

Author

The following guidelines are useful for Author entries.

- Always enter surname first, followed by given names separated by commas:

  Young, Arthur Woods
- Specify the name(s) of the author(s) or editor(s) of a published book, or the author(s) of a periodical or newspaper article. If the work has more than three authors, use *et al.* after the third name.
- Specify an editor as follows:

  Miles, Steven; editor
- Specify the name of the author of a journal, diary, or letter.
- Specify the name of the recorder or transcriber of an interview, audio tape, or video tape.
- Indicate the name of an institution that created a record, index, or database, as follows:

  Vital Statistics, Department of: California, Sacramento

  Sullivan County, New Hampshire: Probate Court

  New Hampshire, Sullivan County: Probate Court

  The Church of Jesus Christ of Latter-day Saints: Salt Lake City, Utah

Publication Information

The following guidelines are useful for Publication Information entries.

You can use codes to tell PAF to print the name of a periodical in italics.

- For a published book, enter the place of publication, name of publisher, and the copyright date, in that order. Include edition number and reprint date if available.
- The title of an article in a periodical is recorded in the Title field enclosed in quotation marks. The name of a periodical should be

italicized, but since there is not a check box to cause the title to be printed in italics, enclose the title in codes using the letter *I*, as follows:

<I>title of periodical</I>

<I>The London Globe</I>

- Enter the name of a periodical or newspaper, along with place of publication, edition number, reprint date, etc.

- For an *unpublished or privately published work*, enter the type or form of the document, such as:

  abstract
  original document
  photocopy
  certified copy
  microfilm, microfiche
  certificate, manuscript, letter
  audio tape, video tape
  e-mail message, e-mail attachment
  original court record
  transcript
  typescript of handwritten copy
  typescript of oral interview
  index of CD-ROM file
  privately published by [name or organization]
  genealogy program used to store database
  software program required to access data

- For an object such as an engraved cup, needlework sampler, or quilt with a family tree that is inscribed with the name, date, and place of an event, include anything known about its origin, manufacture, creation and ownership.

Source Call Number

The following guidelines are useful for Source Call Numbers:

- Enter the library call number or microfilm number if located in a library or archive.

- A source call number is written without *No.* or #, and identifies the source as a book, film, or fiche:

  FHL film British 1234567

- If a film is partitioned into sections called *items*, specify the item number if it contains the entire source. Otherwise, include the range of item numbers.

- If the source includes *multiple* volumes, multiple microfilms, or microfiche, list the range of multiple items available, not just the volume, film, or fiche number used for this source.
- Sometimes one microfiche number *represents a set* with more than one microfiche. When this is the case, indicate how many microfiche are in the set. The same source may then be used for other events with reference to different volumes, films, or microfiche.
- Ensure that the specific volume or film for an event is noted in the Citation Detail section in the Film/Volume/Page Number field.
- If the *source is in a private collection* and has an identifying label, include that information.
- Family researchers should have a system of filing their source documents in a binder, file cabinet or computer. The labels or file names may not be as permanent as in a public archive, but should be noted if available.
- If the *source is in a computer file*, identify the word processing program used, plus the file name and path or an identifying label on a floppy disk. For an Internet site, enter the URL address.

The Actual Text field is not available in PAF 3.

Actual Text

The following guidelines are useful for Actual Text entries:

- The text you want to appear every time you cite the source should be entered in the Actual Text field of the Source description. It will then appear each time you cite that source.
- Examples of actual text in a Source description include the subtitle on a book, the introduction to a church parish record, a one-page text that applies to several individuals, or other text that should accompany the source each time it is cited. For example, consider this full title:

  History of the Town of Stonington, County of New London, Connecticut, from its First Settlement in 1649 to 1900, with a Genealogical Register of Stonington Families.

Source Comments

The following guidelines are useful for Source Comment entries:

- Include anything that will aid in evaluating the source or its contents or will explain the circumstances of creation of the source. For example:

  The original diary, from which the typescript was made, is in the LDS Church Historical Department.

  The subject of the oral interview, Samuel James, was 90 years old, very alert and very easy to understand.

The author gives no sources for this information.

The author is a member of the New England Historic Genealogical Society (NEHGS).

- Describe the condition of the record:

  Book in bad condition, many pages missing.

  Film is nearly illegible.

- Other comments may include information about the original document if the source is an abstract, an index, a typescript, or an original record mentioned in the source. For example:

  The source is an article in a periodical, which gives information about the original record, a parish register of births.

Repository

The following guidelines are useful for *Repository Name* entries:

- Enter the name of the library or archive where the original source was viewed.
- Name the agency or archive holding a transcription or abstract of the original copy.
- Name the person in possession of a book, letter, or other document, even if the person has only a copy of the record. You can list yourself as a repository. Enter the address and telephone number at your discretion.
- Specify the LDS Family History Library in Salt Lake City, Utah, (FHL) if the microfilm or microfiche was borrowed from the FHL, even if it was on indefinite loan to a Family History Center (FHC). It can then be borrowed by another researcher at a different center.
- Specify the FHC if the source document, book, film, or fiche is in the local collection of that FHC, and not available from the FHL.

The following guidelines are useful for *Repository Address* entries:

- If possible, give a street address for a library, archive, or publisher. For the FHL, the address is as follows:

  35 N. West Temple Street, Salt Lake City, UT 84150 USA

- Record only the city of an individual unless you have permission to give the full address. You may want to include the date when the individual was last known to be at that address.
- Since the address is generally used for mailing, the two-letter state abbreviation (U.S. Postal Code) should be used, along with the ZIP code.

Respect the privacy of other individuals.

See Table A-8 for a list of frequently used repository addresses.

- E-mail addresses can be useful to include. However, these addresses frequently change.

The following guidelines are useful for *Repository Telephone* entries:

- Do not give out a telephone number of an individual unless you have permission.
- If you enter a telephone number, be sure you have the area code, or country and city codes.
- The telephone number of the FHL is 1-801-240-2331.

Citation Detail

The following guidelines are useful for *Film/Volume/Page Number* entries:

- Write the source call number without *No.* or #, and identify the source as a book, film, or fiche:

  FHL film British 1234567

- For a film, enter the specific film number if the source covers more than one film. Also enter the item number and, if applicable, the page.
- For a book of more than one volume, enter the specific volume number and the page. Also enter numbers, line numbers, or any other information that would help identify the location within the source.
- If the source has no page numbering, list it as *unpaged.* If possible, indicate an alternate means of locating the source, such as an approximate page, the phrase *chronological order.*
- For a periodical, enter the month and year published, volume, issue number, and page.
- For a newspaper, enter the date and page.
- For an unpublished record, enter the certificate, folio, or other identifying numbers.

Typically you should use the date the record was created.

The following guidelines are useful for *Date entry was made:*

- The *PAF Users Guide* states, "If applicable, type the date the record was made." This is the date the information itself was recorded on the document.
- Do not enter the date on which you are entering the information into your database. Instead, use the date the event itself was recorded in the source.
- If you have a birth or death certificate, enter the date the attending

physician signed the certificate, or if unavailable, the date the certificate was recorded. The actual date the event took place can be added in the Actual Text field in the Citation Detail. If the format of the date differs from that allowed in the date field, the date should be recorded in the Actual Text field.

- If the source is a published book, use the date of publication or the copyright date.
- Enter the publication date of a family Bible since this information could help you evaluate the family records in it.
- If a document does not specify a creation date, but the date can be calculated, enter the calculated date and indicate in the Comments field how the date was derived.

The following guidelines are useful for *Actual Text* entry:

- Text that applies only to a particular individual should be entered in the Citation Detail Actual Text field, so that it appears only on records for that event for that individual.
- Include the actual date of an event as recorded on a certificate, even if the certificate was issued on a different date, or was created long after the date of the original event .
- If a date is recorded in a format that is not allowed in the date field, record it in the Actual Text field. For example:

  Jason died 3 days after Dad's birthday.

- Enter relevant information about the event exactly as it appears in the source. This eliminates the need to return to the source.
- If the actual text is long and difficult to enter, type in an abstract of the text, stating in the Comments field that it is an abstract. Clarify anything in the document that seems confusing.
- Enclose actual text in quotation marks, so that it can be clearly identified as actual text. This is necessary only in PAF 4.

PAF 5 will insert the quotation marks automatically.

- Use square brackets to indicate column headings when transcribing items from columnar forms such as census records, parish records, or forms. (See the example on page 30.)

Square brackets are used to annotate quoted text.

- If you quote a source that contains a footnote or endnote, include the source details of the note.
- Include other relevant information from the document, such as names of parents, cause of death, accuracy of information, legibility of text, use of foreign terms, etc.
- When entering actual text, you may want to precede it by tags.

EDUCATION, RESIDENCE, IMMIGRATION, PARENTS, SIBLINGS, MEDICAL, MILITARY, or OBITUARY are some tags that could be helpful organizing the data and useful in a Focus\Filter search. See Chapter Five for formats.

- If an entry is long and you have a copy of it as a computer file, you can use the Actual Text field to record the computer file name. You can also include a scanned image of the document.

The following guidelines are useful for *Comments* entries:

- Comments can mention the condition or contents of a record.
- The field can contain conflicts and inconsistencies.
- The reliability and accuracy of a record can be noted.
- Estimated or calculated dates should be explained.
- Potentially confusing material can be clarified.
- Indicate the source of place name descriptors, such as *of, upper New York state* or *of, Pocklington, York, England.*
- Tags such as ACTION, CONFLICT, DEADEND, NIL, QUESTION, RESEARCHER, and UPDATE can help categorize a record or situation. These are possible custom tags you can create to guide your research.

Chapter Four: Source Examples

The following hypothetical examples of Source citations are presented as typical circumstances that you might encounter in your research. The elements of the examples follow the fields in the Source template for PAF 3, 4, and 5. In some cases you will find more than one example of a Source Title illustrating the format variations recommended in the guidelines.

Remember that the format of the Source Title will determine the location of the entry in the Source List. To reduce the difficulty in locating the Source entry the next time you wish to attach it to an event, you should use a consistent format throughout.

A typical circumstance for each example is given in the margin to help you understand the details of the example, but they are not intended to be all inclusive. You should be able to find elements of several examples to cover most circumstances you are trying to document.

Please keep in mind that a little documentation is better than nothing.

Chapter Four: Source Entry Examples

Case	Source Entry
1. Ancestral File Extract from CD-ROM	**Source Title:** Ancestral File: CD-ROM; 1998 **Author:** The Church of Jesus Christ of Latter-day Saints **Publication Information:** Set of 9 CD-ROMS **Call Number:** **Repository Name:** [Use location where you normally do research] **Address:** **Telephone:** **Actual Text:** **Comments:** **Citation Detail** **Film/Vol./Page No.:** Ancestral File Number 98K4-GM **Date of Entry:** **Actual Text:** "Louise Reinike, born 15 Oct 1903, New Orleans, Louisiana" **Comments:** **Image:**
2. Ancestral File Extract from the Family-Search® Web site	**Source Title:** Ancestral File: Web version 4.19;1999 **Author:** The Church of Jesus Christ of Latter-day Saints **Publication Information:** Web Site **Call Number:** www.FamilySearch.org **Repository Name:** Family History Department **Address:** 50 East North Temple, Salt Lake City, Utah 84150 **Telephone:** 1-801-240-2190 **Actual Text:** **Comments:** **Citation Detail** **Film/Vol./Page No.:** Ancestral File Number 98K4-GM **Date of Entry:** **Actual Text:** "Louise Reinike, born 15 Oct 1903, New Orleans, Louisiana" **Comments:** accessed 20 Feb 2000 **Image:**

Typical circumstance: Data extracted from the Ancestral Files on CD-ROM at a local Family History Center

Typical circumstance: Birth date and place extracted from the Ancestral file using www.FamilySearch.org on the Web

FamilySearch® is a trademark of Intellectual Reserve, Inc. Salt Lake City.

Chapter Four: Source Entry Examples

Typical Circumstance: Archived Family Group Record with documentation recorded at the bottom of sheet. The letters EMP in the Author field at the end of the Genealogical Society of Utah entry refers to the initials of the researcher.

Typical Circumstance: Family Bible contains birth details

Typical Circumstance: Book contains birth, marriage and children for a family

Case	Source Entry
3. Archive Record	**Source Title:** Ipson Family Records—R. Madsen **Author:** Genealogical Society of Utah: EMP **Publication Information:** Archive Record– Family Group Record compiled for Richard Madsen, Farmington, Utah **Call Number:** **Repository Name:** Jane Black **Address:** **Telephone:** **Actual Text:** **Comments:** Paper records have been microfilmed by the Family History Department, LDS Church; copy in possession of Jane Black.
	Citation Detail **Film/Vol./Page No.:** **Date of Entry:** **Actual Text:** **Comments:** Information obtained from Church records, Census lists: Ellen Christensen, Census 1850 Sonder Hrd 8515 pt 22; Census 1855 Sonder Hrd 8516 pt 38; Census 1860 Sonder Hrd 8517 pt 43; Prob. Rec Sonder Hrd 8775 pt 2 pg 218.
4. Bible, Contains Family Records	**Source Title:** Bible: Samuel Locke Family Bible **or:** Locke, Samuel: Family Bible **Author:** **Publication Information:** Liverpool, England, 1876 **Call Number:** **Repository Name:** Ruth Idlewood **Address:** Snyder, Texas **Telephone:** **Actual Text:** **Comments:** Viewed 13 May 1974 in Snyder, Texas, by Aaron Jones, Santa Clara, California
	Citation Detail **Film/Vol./Page No.:** **Date of Entry:** **Actual Text:** "Births: Samuel Locke, 31 Jan 1881" **Comments:** **Image:**
5. Book, Published	**Source Title:** *Adair County Kentucky Marriages 1801-1850* **Author:** Burdetter, Ruth P.; Compiler **Publication Information:** **Call Number:** US/CAN 987.9 A1 #243 **Repository Name:** Family History Library **Address:** 35 North West Temple, Salt Lake City, Utah 84150 **Telephone:** 1-801-240-3702 **Actual Text:** **Comments:** Transcription from original records
	Citation Detail **Film/Vol./Page No.:** page 14 **Date of Entry:** **Actual Text:** "Boyden, William and Sarah Smith, dau. of William Smith. William son of Joseph Boyden. 15 May 1824." **Comments:** **Image:**

Case	Source Entry
6. Book compiles from other sources	**Source Title:** *Cornwall 1851 Census Liskeard District* **Author:** Woodbine, R.; Transcriber **Publication Information:** Public Record Office Reference Number HO 107/1902, 1994 **Call Number**: FHL Book: British 942.37 X22i volume 2 part 2 **Repository Name:** Family History Library **Address:** 35 North West Temple, Salt Lake City, Utah 84150 **Telephone:** **Actual Text:** **Comments:**
	Citation Detail **Film/Vol./Page No.:** Schedule 117, Folio 0198 & 0199 **Date of Entry:** **Actual Text:** "RICH, William, head,md.,age 44, lead miner, b. St. Neot; Mary, wife, md.,age 40, b. St. Stephens; Charles, son, unmd.,age 20, b. Lanlivery; Jane, daughter, age 7, scholar, b. St. Cleer; William, son, age 4, scholar, b. Liskeard; Richard, son, age 2, b. Liskeard; all living in Church Street North." **Comments:** **Image:**
7. Book, multi-volume set	**Source Title:** *The Great Migration Begins; Immigrants to New England, 1620-1633* **Author:** Anderson, Robert Charles **Publication Information:** Boston: New England Historic Genealogical Society, 1995, 3 Volumes **Call Number:** **Repository Name:** Family History Library **Address:** 35 North West Temple Street, Salt Lake City, Utah 84150 **Telephone:** 1-801-240-3702 **Actual Text:** **Comments:**
	Citation Detail **Film/Vol./Page No.:** Vol. 1, page 47 **Date of Entry:** **Actual Text:** "Anthony Annable, Origin: Cambridge, Cambridge; Migration: 1623 on Anne." **Comments:** **Image:**
8. Book on CD-ROM	**Source Title:** *Arrowheads to Aerojets* **Author:** Flynn, Janet M.; Transcriber **Publication Information:** CD-ROM—Waterloo, Illinois: Monroe County Historical Society, 2000 **Call Number:** **Repository Name:** [Name of Owner] **Address:** [Address of Owner, if permission granted] **Telephone:** **Actual Text:** **Comments:** Book was copyright 1867 by Monroe County, Illinois, Board of Commissioners; edited by Helen Raglan Klein, Gloria Maeys Bundy, Head of Research; Requires Adobe Acrobat Reader. Pictures in the original book are not included.
	Citation Detail **Film/Vol./Page No.:** pg. 202 **Date of Entry:** **Actual Text:** "Jamison, Kathleen; b. 2 Dec 1814" **Comments:** **Image:**

Typical Circumstance: Book compiled from census data

Typical Circumstance: Migration details documented in one volume of a multi-volume compendium of historical data

Typical Circumstance: Out-of-print book published on CD-ROM and sold commercially

Chapter Four: Source Entry Examples

Typical Circumstance: Book published by a private individual and not in general circulation

Typical Circumstance: Cemetery records compiled and published as a book. The entry is similar to a published book

Typical Circumstance: Photo or rubbing of cemetery headstones

Case	Source Entry
9. Book Privately Published	**Source Title:** *First Families of Virginia* **Author:** Robin, Mary **Publication Information:** Privately published, Copyright by Mary Robin, 1978 **Call Number:** **Repository Name:** Henry Jackson **Address:** San Diego, California **Telephone:** **Actual Text:** A Family History and Genealogy covering 350 years, 1620-1970 **Comments:** Contains some sources; copy purchased from the author.
	Citation Detail **Film/Vol./Page No.:** pg. 66 **Date of Entry:** **Actual Text:** "Allen, Martin. c 1775, Bedford County, Virginia. Entered the service of 1812 War at Jonesborough, Tennessee where he had moved with his father's family from Virginia in 1790, as private in Capt. Murray's Co., commanded by Col. Taylor, honorably discharged at Knoxville." **Comments:** See entire biography in Notes tagged BIOGRAPHY.
10. Cemetery Record - Compiled cemetery inscriptions	**Source Title:** *Temple City, Alabama Cemetery Inscriptions* **Author:** Miller, Sydney **Publication Information:** Baltimore: Genealogical Publishing Co., Inc., 1978 **Call Number:** US/CAN 975.6 M56a **Repository Name:** Family History Library **Address:** 35 North West Temple Street, Salt Lake City, Utah **Telephone:** 1-801-240-3702 **Actual Text:** **Comments:**
	Citation Detail **Film/Vol./Page No.:** pg. 129 **Date of Entry:** **Actual Text:** "Charles Lawson 1859-1914" **Comments:** **Image:**
11. Cemetery Record-Headstone Inscription	**Source Title:** Headstone Inscription: Parker, Molly Sarah; Biggs-Gridley Cemetery **or:** Parker, Molly: Headstone Inscription; Biggs-Gridley Cemetery **Author:** Parker, George; photographer **Publication Information:** Photographed Aug 1983 by George Parker **Call Number:** **Repository Name:** Nancy Parker Jackson **Address:** San Jose, California **Telephone:** **Actual Text:** **Comments:** Cemetery located in Gridley, Butte, California
	Citation Detail **Film/Vol./Page No.:** **Date of Entry:** **Actual Text:** "Molly Sarah Parker, 1901-1903" **Comments:** Copy of photograph in possession of Nancy Parker Jackson, San Jose, California **Image:**

Case	Source Entry	
12. Cemetery Record from a Web site	**Source Title:** Cemetery Records: Virginia, Fairfax County, Flint Hill Cemetery **or:** Virginia, Fairfax County: Flint Hill Cemetery **Author:** Cemetery Records On-Line **Publication Information:** Web site **Call Number:** www.interment.net **Repository Name:** **Address:** **Telephone:** **Actual Text:** "This is not a complete listing of burials. The records were provided by contributors to Cemetery Records Online." **Comments:** Extracted details from original cemetery records. **Citation Detail** **Film/Vol./Page No.:** **Date of Entry:** **Actual Text:** "Mintzell, Frederick "Fritz" b. Jul 16, 1894, d. Jan 11, 1984 h/o Mabel C. Croson, [LC]"	*Typical Circumstance:* Birth and death details extracted from cemetery records and published on a Web site
13. Census Record - On CD-ROM	**Source Title:** Census: Tennessee, Washington County; 1870 U.S. Federal **or:** 1870 U.S. Federal Census: Tennessee, Washington County **or:** Tennessee, Washington County: 1870 U.S. Federal Census **Author:** Family Quest Archives **Publication Information:** Heritage Quest, a division of AGLL. Inc., 1998 **Call Number:** M593-1568 **Repository Name:** Ann Lenning **Address:** San Diego, California **Telephone:** **Actual Text:** **Comments:** Scanned images of the actual census **Citation Detail** **Film/Vol./Page No.:** pg. 324 **Date of Entry:** **Actual Text:** "William Walker, age 45, male, white, farmer, born: North Carolina." **Comments:** Images are highly legible	*Typical Circumstance:* Census records extracted and published commercially
14. Census data published on a Web site	**Source Title:** Census: 1880 United States **or:** 1880 United States Census **or:** United States: 1880 Census **Author:** The Church of Jesus Christ of Latter-day Saints **Publication Information:** Web site **Call Number:** www.FamilySearch.org **Repository Name:** Family History Department **Address:** 50 East North Temple, Salt Lake City, Utah **Telephone:** **Actual Text:** **Comments:** Census data extracted from original census records **Citation Detail** **Film/Vol./Page No.:** FHL Film 1255336 NA Film No. T9-1336 Page 207C **Date of Entry:** **Actual Text:** "Henrietta C. Call, Birth Year <1827>, Birthplace: NY, Age: 53, Occupation: [blank], Marital Status: W <Widowed>, Race: W <White>, Head of Household: Henriett C. Call, Relation: Self, Father's Birthplace: CT, Mother's birthplace: VT." **Comments:**	*Typical Circumstance:* Census data extracted from census published on a Web site

Chapter Four: Source Entry Examples

Typical Circumstance: Census record on microfilm showing family and possible supplementary information

Typical Circumstance: Non-U.S. Census record with illegible information

Typical Circumstance: Census index published commercially on CD-ROM

Case	Source Entry
15. Census Record - on micro film	**Source Title:** Census, U.S. Federal: California; 1900 **or:** 1900 U.S. Federal Census: California **or:** California: 1900 U.S. Federal Census **Author:** US Census Breau **Publication Information:** Microfilm **Call Number:** T623 number 81-116 **Repository Name:** Federal Records Archives Center **Address:** 1000 Commodore Drive, San Bruno, California **Telephone:** 1-650-876-9009 **Actual Text:** **Comments:**
	Citation Detail **Film/Vol./Page No.:** Roll T1032 Roll 85; Vol 45, E.D. 54 Sheet 17; Line 2 **Date of Entry:** 14 Jul 1900 **Actual Text:** "Robert Call, head, male, age 45, married, farmer, born: Kentucky, father born: Virginia; mother born: North Carolina." **Comments:** Living next door to William Call, age 42, born: Kentucky; possibly a brother.
16. Census Record - Non-U.S.	**Source Title:** England, Cornwall: 1841 British Census **or:** Census, British: England, Cornwall, 1841 **or:** Census, British: 1841 England, Cornwall **Author:** British Government **Publication Information:** Microfilm **Call Number:** FHL Film 1453699-1456872 **Repository Name:** Family History Library **Address:** **Telephone:** **Actual Text:** **Comments:** Film is light and difficult to read.
	Citation Detail **Film/Vol./Page No.:** FHL Film 1453704, Liskeard District, St. Cleer Parish, piece number 45, folio number 16 **Date of Entry:** 8 Jul 1841 **Actual Text:** "St. Cleer, Cornwall, Rosradd…, Charles Higgs, age 80, …; Ann (do)., age 60, William (do)., age 35, labr. in …, Elizabeth (do), age 6, all born in parish." **Comments:** Illegible portions indicated in actual text by "…"
17. Census Index Record	**Source Title:** Census Index: U.S. Selected State / Counties; 1870 **or:** Census Index: 1870 U.S. Selected State / Counties **Author:** The Learning Company **Publication Information:** Broderbund Family Archive, CD-ROM **Call Number:** No. 320, Ed. 1 **Repository Name:** Nancy Allen **Address:** Los Angeles, California **Telephone:** **Actual Text:** **Comments:**
	Citation Detail **Film/Vol./Page No.:** Doddridge County, West Virginia **Date of Entry:** **Actual Text:** "Dobbs, Henry, pg. 356, Henshaw Twp." **Comments:** **Image:**

Case	Source Entry	
18. Church Record on microfilm	**Source Title:** Parish Register: England, Cornwall, St. Neot Parish **or:** England, Cornwall: St. Neot Parish Register **Author:** Anglican Church **Publication Information:** Microfilm, Genealogical Society of Utah, 1989 **Call Number:** FHL Film 1596065, Items 7-14 and 1596066, Items 1-3 **Repository Name:** Family History Library **Address:** 35 North Temple Street, Salt Lake City, Utah 84150 **Telephone:** 1-801-240-3702 **Actual Text:** **Comments:** **Citation Detail** **Film/Vol./Page No.:** FHL Film 1596065 Items 7-14, pg. 138 **Date of Entry:** **Actual Text:** "William Son of Charles & Elizabeth Smith was baptized 27 July 1806." **Comments:** **Image:**	*Typical Circumstance:* Church Record on microfilm
19. Church Record - Non-English record	**Source Title:** Nieder Weisel, Ober-Hessen: Parish Registers **or:** Parish Registers: Nieder Weisel, Ober-Hessen **Author:** Evangelische Kirche (Protestant Church) **Publication Information:** Microfilm, Genealogical Society of Utah, 1971 **Call Number:** FHL Film 1269949-1269952 **Repository Name:** Family History Library **Address:** 35 North West Temple Salt Lake City, Utah 84150 **Telephone:** 1-801-240-3702 **Actual Text:** **Comments:** Microfilm of original parish records; legible copy. **Citation Detail** **Film/Vol./Page No.:** FHL Film 1269949 Births 1690-1761 chron **Date of Entry:** **Actual Text:** (Translated from German) (1708) "On the 6th of October was Anna, Conrad Bill's wife, born Rumpf, delivered of a son for whom the master smith Johann Hildbrand was godfather." **Comments:** **Image:**	*Typical Circumstance:* Birth event recorded in a parish register in a non-English language
20. City Directory	**Source Title:** London Trade Directory, 1870 **Author:** **Publication Information:** London: Harpers Publishing, 1870 **Call Number:** HO 45/12 **Repository Name:** Public Records Office **Address:** Ruskin Ave. Kew, Surrey, England TW9 4DU **Telephone:** 0181 876 3444 **Actual Text:** **Comments:** Contains business addresses for central London only **Citation Detail** **Film/Vol./Page No.:** Page 46 **Date of Entry:** **Actual Text:** "34 Oxford St., Jacobs and Sons, Master Cobblers. Samuel and sons, Isaac and Levi at your service." **Comments:** **Image:**	*Typical Circumstance:* Family relationship is noted by an entry in a business directory

Chapter Four: Source Entry Examples

Typical Circumstance: Official adoption record filed at the county recorders office and photocopy in family records

Typical Circumstance: Information about the birth of a child taken from the mother's personal diary

Typical Circumstance: Information received via e-mail from another researcher with a documented source

Case	Source Entry
21. Court Record, Adoption	**Source Title:** Judgment of Adoption for Susannah Wilson Hoyle **Author:** County Clerk **Publication Information:** Santa Clara County, California, 1991 **Call Number:** **Repository Name:** County Recorders Office **Address:** 70 West Hedding Ave., San Jose, California 95114 **Telephone:** 1-408-299-2481 **Actual Text:** **Comments:**
	Citation Detail **Film/Vol./Page No.:** Petition Number A12345 **Date of Entry:** filed 15 Jan 1991 **Actual Text:** Actual document is 8 pages, stating that Susannah is the legally adopted child of Nathan and Nancy Hoyle **Comments:** Photocopy of judgment in possession of Nathan Hoyle **Image:**
22. Personal Diary	**Source Title:** Diary: Pearlman, Hattie (1887-1892) **or** Perlman, Hattie: Diary **Author:** Perlman, Hattie **Publication Information:** Handwritten personal diary covering 4 Jan 1887 to 19 Dec 1892 **Call Number:** **Repository Name:** [Personal address] **Address:** **Telephone:** **Actual Text:** **Comments:** Diary is legible, but pages are loose. Dates on each page maintain page sequence
	Citation Detail **Film/Vol./Page No.:** Page dated 13 April 1888 **Date of Entry:** **Actual Text:** "On Wednesday the 9th of this month, I gave birth to my second daughter, Cassie." **Comments:** **Image:**
23. E-mail Message containing family data	**Source Title:** Family Records: Fry, Michael **or:** Fry, Michael: Family Records **Author:** Winter, James **Publication Information:** e-mail message from <jkfry@best.net>, received 8 Feb 2000 **Call Number:** **Repository Name:** Joan Winter **Address:** 876 North Lane, Cincinnati, Ohio **Telephone:** **Actual Text:** **Comments:** Michael Fry extracted this information from a microfilm of original parish records; legible copy.
	Citation Detail **Film/Vol./Page No.:** **Date of Entry:** **Actual Text:** "James Winter immigrated to U.S. in 1848 from Bohemia." **Comments:** **Image:**

Case	Source Entry
24. Family Records, Collection of misc. records	**Source Title:** Family Records: Rosewood, Thomas Wilde **Author:** Small, Richard Kimball; compiler **Publication Information:** Unpublished collection of miscellaneous records **Call Number:** **Repository Name:** Small, Richard Kimball **Address:** Montreal, Quebec, Canada **Telephone:** **Actual Text:** **Comments:** Material is organized alphabetically by surname in four drawers of a black metal filing cabinet. Thomas Wilde Rosewood is the grandfather of Richard Kimball Small.
	Citation Detail **Film/Vol./Page No.:** Birth Certificate: Rosewood, Gloria **Date of Entry:** 8 Jan 1931 **Actual Text:** "Daughter, Gloria, born Jan. 5, 1931 to Jacob Rosewood and Mary." **Comments:** Certificate appears to be the original document issued at Portneuf, Quebec, Canada on 8 Jan 1931. **Image:**
25. Family History scrapbook	**Source Title:** The Roots of the Palgraves, A Family History **or:** Palgrave: The Roots of the Palgraves, A Family History **Author:** Palmer, Josephine, compiler **Publication Information:** An unpublished scrapbook compiled between 1941-45 **Call Number:** **Repository Name:** Gilbert Palmer **Address:** 34 Haymarket St., Bedminster, England **Telephone:** **Actual Text:** **Comments:** A compilation of family history compiled from various family diaries and journals
	Citation Detail **Film/Vol./Page No.:** **Date of Entry:** 1941-1945 **Actual Text:** "Thomas Palgrave was christened at St. Mark's Chapel [Bristol, Gloucester, England] on 23 March 1796." **Comments:** Most of the material on Thomas Palgrave appears to have been gathered from lost diaries written by his son, William. **Image:**
26. Data extracted from the IGI on CD-ROM	**Source Title:** International Genealogical Index (IGI): CD-ROM, version 1.01 **Author:** The Church of Jesus Christ of Latter-day Saints **Publication Information:** CD-ROM: 34 discs plus 17 supplementary discs; 1997 **Call Number:** **Repository Name:** [Enter your local repository] **Address:** **Telephone:** **Actual Text:** **Comments:**
	Citation Detail **Film/Vol./Page No.:** **Date of Entry:** **Actual Text:** "Jasper Randall, born abt 1576, of Hampshire, England." **Comments:** **Image:**

Typical Circumstance: Family Historian with a large collection of miscellaneous family records organized by surnames

Typical Circumstance: Material compiled into a Family History scrapbook

Typical Circumstance: Data extracted from the IGI on CD-ROMs at a local Family History Center

Chapter Four: Source Entry Examples

Typical Circumstance: Data extracted from the Internet IGI at www.FamilySearch.org

Typical Circumstance: Details extracted from the Passenger Records at www.ellisisland.org

Typical Circumstance: Names and ages annotated on a photograph

Case	Source Entry
27. Data extracted from the Internet IGI	**Source Title:** International Genealogical Index (IGI): Web Site, 2002 **Author:** The Church of Jesus Christ of Latter-day Saints **Publication Information:** Web site **Call Number:** www.FamilySearch.org **Repository Name:** Family History Department **Address:** 50 East North Temple, Salt Lake City, Utah, 84150-3400 **Telephone:** **Actual Text:** **Comments:**
	Citation Detail **Film/Vol./Page No.:** Film Batch No. C112823 Source Call No. 6035516 **Date of Entry:** **Actual Text:** "Charles Leonard Lindberg; Birth: 24 Mar 1871 Dundee, Angus, Scotland" **Comments:** Region: British Isles (1868-1875)
28. Immigration record, Ellis Island	**Source Title:** Ellis Island On-Line **Author:** The Statue of Liberty-Ellis Island Foundation, Inc. **Publication Information:** Web site **Call Number:** www.EllisIsland.org **Repository Name:** **Address:** **Telephone:** **Actual Text:** **Comments:** Site contains immigration records from Ellis Island between 1892 and 1924
	Citation Detail **Film/Vol./Page No.:** Page # 0117 Line 11 Ship's Manifest **Date of Entry:** **Actual Text:** "Name: Randall, Thos. Richard; Ethnicity: Eng., Brit.; Date of Arrival: September 15, 1920; Age on Arrival: 16y; Gender: M; Ship of travel: Olympic; Port of Departure: Southampton, Southamptonshire, England, UK. A member of the ship's crew." **Comments:**
29. Image from a photo album	**Source Title:** Family Records: Brigham, Janet **Author:** **Publication Information:** Unpublished collection of documents, photos, correspondence, and certificates for ancestral history **Call Number:** **Repository Name:** [personal address] **Address:** **Telephone:** **Actual Text:** **Comments:** Jensen family photos, blessings, and correspondence
	Citation Detail **Film/Vol./Page No.:** **Date of Entry:** about 1891 **Actual Text:** "[Annotation on back of photo:] Sibyl 5—May 2" **Comments:** Mounted studio photo of Sibyl Jensen, age 5, and her sister, May Jensen, age 2, with photographer's logo: Lewis & Allen, Second Street, Logan, Utah **Image:**

Case	Source Entry
30. Land Record	**Source Title:** Deed of Sale: Lynch, Jacob to Nielsen, Robert **Author:** County Recorder **Publication Information:** Filmed by the Wabash Valley Genealogical Society, 1971 **Call Number:** Microfilm L78-5 **Repository Name:** Wabash Valley Genealogical Society **Address:** P.O. Box 85, Terre Haute, Indiana 47808 **Telephone:** **Actual Text:** **Comments:** Film contains assorted public records including probate and deeds
	Citation Detail **Film/Vol./Page No.:** Page 102 **Date of Entry:** 23 Jan 1848 **Actual Text:** Lot described in deed "sold by Jacob Lynch for $35 on 23 Jan 1848." **Comments:** The deed lends proof that Jacob Lynch left Indiana in Jan. 1848 and moved to Fort Laramie, Wyoming. **Image:**
31. Letter, Private Correspondence	**Source Title:** Family Records: Harris, Robert Long **or:** Langley, Joseph: Personal Correspondence; 1861 **Author:** Harris, Robert Long; compiler **or:** Langley, Joseph **Publication Information:** Miscellaneous unpublished documents **Call Number:** **Repository Name:** Robert Long Harris **Address:** 1239 Vista Knoll Lane, Bedford, England **Telephone:** **Actual Text:** **Comments:**
	Citation Detail **Film/Vol./Page No.:** **Date of Entry:** **Actual Text:** "Grandfather Nathan [Langley] died last Tuesday morning [19 Mar 1861] after a long struggle with black lung disease." **Comments:** Letter dated 23 Mar 1861 written by Joseph Langley to a cousin . 23 Mar 1861 is a Sunday which would make the previous Tuesday the 19th. Photocopy of letter in possession of Robert Long Harris. **Image:**
32. Lineage Society	**Source Title:** Pioneer Women of Faith and Fortitude: Vol III **Author:** International Society Daughters of Utah Pioneers **Publication Information:** Salt Lake City: Publishers Press, 1998 **Call Number:** **Repository Name:** Carol Harless **Address:** **Telephone:** **Actual Text:** **Comments:**
	Citation Detail **Film/Vol./Page No.:** Page 2488 **Date of Entry:** **Actual Text:** Sarah Anderson Rands (heading title) **Comments:** Entry lists husband, Joseph William Rands, and nine children. Includes a photo and nearly a full page biography of Sarah. **Image:**

Typical Circumstance: The date of a deed adds details to other documents connecting two families that appear to be the same

Typical Circumstance: A copy of a letter written by a close relative noting the death of an individual with sufficient details to determine the probable date death date

Typical Circumstance: Compilation of descendents of a noted society or group contains biography of individual

Chapter Four: Source Entry Examples

Case	Source Entry
33. Manu-script, Unpub-lished *Typical Circumstance:* Unpublished copy of a manuscript containing oral history of family	**Source Title:** *Genealogy of the Harmon Family* **Author:** Harmon, Mary Ann **Publication Information:** Unpublished manuscript dictated by Mary Ann Harmon to her son, William, in 1894 **Call Number:** **Repository Name:** John Black **Address:** 321 Main Street, Reno, Nevada 84125 **Telephone:** 1-350-555-1435 **Actual Text:** **Comments:** Mary Ann was said to have a very good memory for names and dates. She dictated the information from her memory and most of the data has been confirmed with other sources to be correct. **Citation Detail** **Film/Vol./Page No.:** pg. 2 **Date of Entry:** 1894 **Actual Text:** "Meshack Harmon, born 1829 in Washington County, Tennessee" **Comments:**
34. Marriage Record *Typical Circumstance:* Original Marriage Certificate containing date and place of marriage	**Source Title:** McKinley, Leonard Ashley: Marriage Certificate **or:** Family Records: Randolph, Harold T. **Author:** County Recorder **or:** Randolph, Harold T.; compiler **Publication Information:** Miscellaneous unpublished documents **Call Number:** **Repository Name:** Harold Randolph **Address:** 432 Princess Court, Pasadena, California **Telephone:** **Actual Text:** **Comments:** **Citation Detail** **Film/Vol./Page No.:** Certified Certificate of Marriage **Date of Entry:** 18 May 1930 **Actual Text:** "...on May 18 1930 at Union Hall, Evanston, Wyoming...Leonard Ashley McKinley was joined in marriage to Donna Strebel..." **Comments:** Original certificate in possession of Harold Randolph
35. Military Service Record *Typical Circumstance:* Official military discharge certificate indicating period of service and reason for discharge	**Source Title:** Military Service Record: Mulkeme, George Antone (1932) **or:** Mulkeme, George Antone (1932): Military Service Record **Author:** U.S. Department of the Air Force—Regular Air Force **Publication Information:** Certified Copy Number 2 of DD (Dept. of Defense), Form 214, Certificate of Release or Discharge from Active Duty **Call Number:** **Repository Name:** National Personnel Records Center **Address:** Military Personnel Records, 9700 Page Ave., St. Louis, MO 63132-5100 **Telephone:** **Actual Text:** **Comments:** Contains summary of service record from date and place entered active duty to date and place of separation. **Citation Detail** **Film/Vol./Page No.:** Marked "Service—2", meaning second official copy **Date of Entry:** Originally on or about 31 Jul 1981, copy certified on 18 Nov 1998 **Actual Text:** "Item 28: Narrative Reason for Separation: Vol-Retirement for years of service established by law." **Comments:** **Image:**

Case	Source Entry
36. Newspaper Article — Obituary	**Source Title:** "Obituaries: Wilson, Georgina (Mason)" **Author:** Mercury News, San Jose, California **Publication Information:** <I>San Jose Mercury News</I> **Call Number:** **Repository Name:** Santa Clara County Library **Address:** 2635 Homestead Ave., Santa Clara, CA **Telephone:** 1-408-984-3236 **Actual Text:** **Comments:**
	Citation Detail **Film/Vol./Page No.:** Microfilm, SJ Mercury News — Sept-Nov 1943 **Date of Entry:** 16 Oct 1943 **Actual Text:** "Wilson, Georgina (Mason) - died peacefully Oct. 13, 1943, age 76 in Sunnyvale, California. She is survived by her only son, Jerome Wilson." **Comments:** **Image:**
37. Newspaper clipping, no known source	**Source Title:** "Triple the Fun, Shelly Family Gets Big Fast" **Author:** Shelly, Marcia; compiler **Publication Information:** Unknown newspaper **Call Number:** **Repository Name:** [owner of clipping] **Address:** **Telephone:** **Actual Text:** **Comments:** Clipping on page 34 of scrapbook compiled by Marcia Shelly
	Citation Detail **Film/Vol./Page No.:** **Date of Entry:** About Nov 1907 **Actual Text:** "...Hannah Shelly gave birth to triplets Saturday evening. John reported that mother and children are doing fine. The daughter was named Suzannah, and the two boys will be named Harold and Joseph." **Comments:** The clipping contains no indication of the source, but may have been from the Detroit Free Press. **Image:**
38. Oral Interview	**Source Title:** Oral Interview: Jones, Mary; 1972 **Author:** Jones, Aaron; Interviewer **Publication Information:** Recorded on tape cassette, 2 Jun 1972 **Call Number:** **Repository Name:** Aaron Jones **Address:** 789 Homestead Rd., Calgary, Alberta, Canada **Telephone:** **Actual Text:** [Interview contains birth dates, marriages, and deaths of Mary's extended family] **Comments:** Interview recorded in Santa Cruz, California, when Mary was age 71. Recording made using a cassette tape.
	Citation Detail **Film/Vol./Page No.:** **Date of Entry:** **Actual Text:** "Harold was born on the 4th of July, 1913 in Hamilton, Ontario.." **Comments:** Comment occurs when Mary is describing her parents. **Image:**

Typical Circumstance: Obituary published in a newspaper with useful information about surviving family

Typical Circumstance: Old newspaper clipping found in a scrapbook or diary without the date or newspaper's name shown

Typical Circumstance: Lengthy recorded interview with parent who knew by heart all the birth dates, places, marriages, and deaths of her extended family

Chapter Four: Source Entry Examples

Typical Circumstance: Ordinance information indexed on CD-ROM

Case	Source Entry
39. Ordinance Index showing baptism	**Source Title:** Ordinance Index: Version 1 **Author:** The Church of Jesus Christ of Latter-day Saints **Publication Information:** CD-ROM **Call Number:** **Repository Name:** Family History Library **Address:** 35 North West Temple Street, Salt Lake City, Utah **Telephone:** **Actual Text:** **Comments:** Information accessed using FamilySearch computer program
	Citation Detail **Film/Vol./Page No.:** **Date of Entry:** before October 1997 **Actual Text:** "Ba: 5010022; So: 1553419" **Comments:** Printout of data in possession of Jane Black; source of data in Actual Text field **Image:**
40. Ordiance Record, from Internet IGI	**Source title:** FamilySearch International Genealogical Index v5.0 **or:** Web Site: FamilySearch International Genealogical Index v5.0 **Author:** The Church of Jesus Christ of Latter-day Saints **Publication Information:** Web Site **Call Number:** www.FamilySearch.org **Repository Name:** Family History Library **Address:** 35 North West Temple Street, Salt Lake City, Utah **Telephone:** **Actual Text:** **Comments:**
	Citation Detail **Film/Vol./Page No.:** Film Batch No: M972401 Source Call No. 0488340 **Date of Entry:** **Actual Text:** "Jacobus Ropert, Sealing to Spouse: 27 Feb 1992 IFALL, [Spouse] Elisabetha Wigenhouser" **Comments:** Accessed 11 May 2002, 7:30 pm PST by James Hassenbach **Image:**
41. Pedigree Resource File, CD-ROM	**Source Title:** Pedigree Resource File: 1999 **Author:** Church of Jesus Christ of Latter-day Saints **Publication Information:** CD-ROM **Call Number:** **Repository Name:** [Use location where you normally do research] **Address:** (or name of owner of CD set) **Telephone:** **Actual Text:** **Comments:** CD-ROM available at most Family History Centers
	Citation Detail **Film/Vol./Page No.:** Pedigree Resource File, CD-ROM 5 **Date of Entry:** 1999-2000 **Actual Text:** "Hansen, Josephine; born 5 Nov 1860, Drypool, Yorkshire, England." **Comments:** (indicate source of information, or specify if none is listed) **Image:**

Typical Circumstance: LDS Ordinance dates extracted from Internet IGI at www.FamilySearch.org

Typical Circumstance: Data extracted from the Pedigree Resource File on CD-ROM

Case	Source Entry
42. Pedigree Resource File, Web site	**Source title:** Pedigree Resource File **Author:** The Church of Jesus Christ of Latter-day Saints **Publication Information:** Web site **Call Number:** www.FamilySearch.org **Repository Name:** Family History Department **Address:** 50 East North Temple, Salt Lake City, Utah **Telephone:** **Actual Text:** **Comments:** Accessed using Internet Explorer. **Citation Detail** **Film/Vol./Page No.:** CD-ROM #6 Pin # 791275 **Date of Entry:** **Actual Text:** "Thomas Powell Winter, Birth: abt 1763 Place: N. Petherton, Smrst [Somerset], ENG [England]" **Comments:** Accessed 15 Nov 2002 8:45 pm PST **Image:**
43. Periodical with a Source within a Source	**Source Title:** "The English Ancestors of Joshua and Anthony Fisher" **Author:** Hyde, Myrtle Stevens and Plummer, John **Publication Information:** <I>New England Historical and Genealogical Register</I>, Vol 151, April 1997 **Call Number:** **Repository Name:** [name of owner] **Address:** **Telephone:** **Actual Text:** **Comments:** This is a well documented study of English records, some taken from FHL microfilm. Problems with previously published records are reviewed. **Citation Detail** **Film/Vol./Page No.:** pg. 178, 182 **Date of Entry:** **Actual Text:** "Syleham, Suffolk, England parish register transcript; S. E. H. Aldwell, ed., 1936; FHL microfilm 991, 994, item 22." **Comments:** **Image:**
44. Personal Knowl-edge	**Source Title:** Personal Knowledge: Hannover, Joshua Blye **Author:** Hannover, Joshua Blye **Publication Information:** **Call Number:** **Repository Name:** Joshua Hannover **Address:** Munich, Germany **Telephone:** **Actual Text:** **Comments:** Personal knowledge of undocumented information **Citation Detail** **Film/Vol./Page No.:** **Date of Entry:** **Actual Text:** **Comments:** All known documentation destroyed during WW II, but Joshua Hannover clearly remembers birth date and place. **Image:**

Typical Circumstance: Data extracted from the Pedigree Resource File at FamilySearch.org

Typical Circumstance: Article in a periodical containing information extracted from another source

Typical Circumstance: Lacking original documentation, the best available source is a close family member who vouches for the details

Chapter Four: Source Entry Examples

Typical Circumstance: Object containing inscribed information pertaining to an event is only known proof of birth data

Typical Circumstance: Probate record contains a dated will with the names and ages of the entire family, including spouses, allowing calculation of approximate birth dates

Typical Circumstance: Detailed report created by a professional research organization on request from your family.

Case	Source Entry
45. Personal Object with inscription	**Source Title:** Kelly, Patrick Sullivan (1902): silver cup **or:** Silver cup, inscribed: Kelly, Patrick Sullivan **Author:** **Publication Information:** **Call Number:** **Repository Name:** Patrick Sullivan Kelly III **Address:** Boston, Massachusetts **Telephone:** **Actual Text:** **Comments:** A sterling silver cup that has been passed down from son to grandson
	Citation Detail **Film/Vol./Page No.:** **Date of Entry:** **Actual Text:** "Patrick Sullivan Kelly, Born New York City, March 17, 1902." **Comments:** Information is engraved on the side of the cup which contains the following trademark: Tiffany & Co. Sterling Silver **Image:**
46. Probate Record	**Source Title:** Probate Packet: Mitchell, Lawrence; 1846 **or:** Mitchell, Lawrence: Probate Packet; 1846 **Author:** County Clerk **Publication Information:** County Records, Sullivan County, New Hampshire **Call Number:** **Repository Name:** County Court Records Archive **Address:** P.O. Box 45, Newport, New Hampshire **Telephone:** **Actual Text:** **Comments:** Copy obtained by correspondence with County Clerk contains names and ages of the entire Lawrence Mitchell family, including spouses. Photocopy in possession of Harriet Mitchell Brown of Providence, Rhode Island
	Citation Detail **Film/Vol./Page No.:** Page 2 **Date of Entry:** 6 Jun 1846 **Actual Text:** "Will dated 3 Aug 1838; probate settled 6 Jun 1846; Lawrence Mitchell died 17 Apr 1846 in Newport, New Hampshire." **Comments:** **Image:**
47. Research Report, created by a professional research organization	**Source title:** Research Report: (IGS 3689) **Author:** Anderson, Herbert; compiler **Publication Information:** International Genealogy Services, 1992 **Call Number:** **Repository Name:** Christian Olson **Address:** Henderson, Nevada **Telephone:** **Actual Text:** **Comments:** A nine-page report researched and compiled for Christian Olson, commissioned on 13 Jan 1992
	Citation Detail **Film/Vol./Page No.:** Page 6 **Date of Entry:** **Actual Text:** "Christensen, Ole b: May 04, 1824 in Ramnes, Vestfold, Norway d: December 22, 1902 in Ogden, Weber, Utah." **Image:**

Case	Source Entry
48. Social Security Death Index	**Source title:** U.S. Social Security Death Index: CD-ROM; 1997 **Author:** U.S. Social Security Administration **Publication Information:** Set of 2 CD-ROMS published May 1997 by LDS Church **Call Number:** **Repository Name:** [Local Family History Center] **Address:** **Telephone:** **Actual Text:** **Comments:** Accessed using FamilySearch program. Files contain data from Master Death Index through Dec. 1996
	Citation Detail **Film/Vol./Page No.:** **Date of Entry:** **Actual Text:** "Harold Tingey, born 4 Dec 1897; died Aug 1969, Nutley, Essex, New Jersey." **Comments:** **Image:**
49. Vital Records Index	**Source title:** Vital Records Index: North America, Kentucky, Hopkins **or:** Kentucky, Hopkins: Vital Records Index, North America **Author:** The Church of Jeses Christ of Latter-day Saints **Publication Information:** Family History Resource File, set of 7 discs **Call Number:** **Repository Name:** [Local Family History Center or owner of CD-ROMs] **Address:** **Telephone:** **Actual Text:** **Comments:**
	Citation Detail **Film/Vol./Page No.:** Disc 1 Births/Christenings **Date of Entry:** **Actual Text:** "Williams, William [Birth Date:] 15 Oct 1853 [Birthplace:] Hopkins county, Ky. [Source:] FHL Number 216824 [Dates:] 1852-1859" **Comments:** **Image:**
50. Web site, direct access	**Source title:** Kennedy Family: Web Site **or:** Web Site: Kennedy Family **Author:** Kennedy, John; webmaster <jk@best.net> **Publication Information:** Internet Web Site **Call Number:** <www.kennedy.com> **Repository Name:** John Kennedy **Address:** 456 Main St., Dallas, Texas 79465 **Telephone:** **Actual Text:** **Comments:** Contains history of the Kennedy family of Massachusetts, 1750-1989
	Citation Detail **Film/Vol./Page No.:** page 9 **Date of Entry:** **Actual Text:** "Benjamin Kennedy, b. 5 May 1845, Boston, Massachusetts." **Comments:** Downloaded 11 May 1999, 7:30 pm PST by John Kennedy **Image:**

Typical Circumstance: Death information specified in the Social Security Death Index available on CD-ROM

Typical Circumstance: Birth details extracted from a CD-ROM collection.

Typical Circumstance: Information extracted from a Web site.

Chapter Four: Source Entry Examples

Typical Circumstance: A GEDCOM file was downloaded from a general purpose web site

Typical Circumstance: The original Will listing the names, married names, and ages of children, including some members of the extended family.

Typical Circumstance: Entry in school yearbook documenting education, residence, approximate age, and extracurricular interests.

Case	Source Entry
51. Web Site, GEDCOM file download	**Source title:** Descendants of Lewis Owen Of Llwyn And Plas-Yn-Dre, Dolgelley **Author:** Warner, Crystal Lynn (Owen); compiler **Publication Information:** Web Site **Call Number:** www.familytreemaker.com/users/w/a/r/Crystal-L-Warner/index.html **Repository Name:** Crystal Lynn (Owen) Warner **Address:** Louisville, Kentucky **Telephone:** **Actual Text:** **Comments:** Site contains 58 pages of descendency charts with GEDCOM file download available
	Citation Detail **Film/Vol./Page No.:** Page 55 **Date of Entry:** **Actual Text:** "Harold Robert Randall b: May 04, 1924 in Centerville, Davis, Utah d: December 22, 1926 in Ogden, Weber, Utah." **Image:**
52. Will, original copy documenting names and ages of heirs	**Source title:** Will: Young, Matthew **or:** Young, Matthew: Will **Author:** Young, Matthew **Publication Information:** Prerogative Court of Canterbury **Call Number:** PC: 270Y61 **Repository Name:** Suffolk County Public Records Office **Address:** Ipswitch, Suffolk, England **Telephone:** **Actual Text:** **Comments:** Contains an Inventory of Matthew Young's estate at Debenham and the administration of a bequest to extended family members.
	Citation Detail **Film/Vol./Page No.:** page 4 **Date of Entry:** 23 Aug 1813 **Actual Text:** "...to my son-in-law, Jason Peters..." **Comments:** At the date of the will, Katherine was the only child of marriage-able age. It is assumed that Jason is Katherine's husband. **Image:**
53. Yearbook, school	**Source title:** Bellendaine (1960) **Author:** Hartman, Janet; editor **Publication Information:** Monrovia, California: Yearbooks Incorporated **Call Number:** Special Collections **Repository Name:** Glendora Public Library **Address:** Glendora, California **Telephone:** **Actual Text:** **Comments:** Glendora High School Yearbook, Glendora, California. No index of individuals
	Citation Detail **Film/Vol./Page No.:** Page 55 **Date of Entry:** May 1960 **Actual Text:** "[Graduating Class entry] Susan Smolter, Drama Club 3" **Image:**

Chapter Five: How to Create Notes

Since PAF 3, PAF 4, and PAF 5 provide a method for documenting sources separate from recording notes, users now have more freedom in using the notes feature. However, a consistent format is still recommended for entering notes in your database. Because the recommendations published earlier by the Silicon Valley PAF Users Group have become widely accepted, many programs that complement PAF have been developed with the format of PAF notes in mind. So even though source documentation should no longer to be entered as notes, other information that is entered as notes should follow a consistent format. We recommend a format similar to that suggested in the earlier guidelines.

To open the Notes screen, click on the *Notes* icon on the Edit Individual window. You can also access the Notes screen for an individual highlighted on the Family, Pedigree, or Individual view on your screen using the *Notes* option in the *Edit* pull-down menu. In PAF 5 you may right-click on an individual's name on any of the three screen formats, *Family*, *Pedigree*, or *Individual*, and select Notes to access the Edit Notes screen. If you have not set the option to use the Notes Selector feature, the Notes screen will appear. The Notes screen is a blank screen that does not require any specific syntax or format. Enter your notes as if you were typing information on a blank sheet of paper. Once you have entered a note, the Notes icon will have an asterisk (*) attached to it.

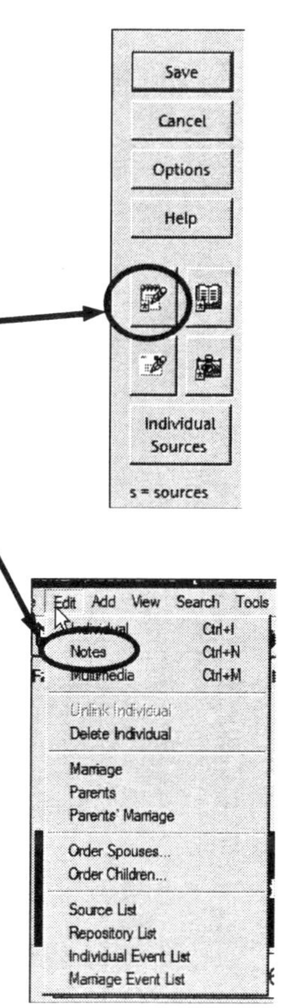

If you have the Notes Selector feature turned on, the Notes Selector window will pop up first. For more information about the Notes Selector feature, go to the end of this Chapter.

A Note entry will consist of a block of text that is formatted for consistency and clarity. If you use the recommendations below, your notes will be readily understandable by others, and the Notes Selector system will work for you.

Field Description

Note Significance Character

This is the first character of a note. There are three ways to indicate the significance of a note:

- **Tilde Character (~) for Confidential Notes —** PAF 4 and 5 allow the use of the tilde character as a means for marking a note as confidential. When you are printing reports or exporting data to a GEDCOM file and you indicate that notes are to be included,

~ADOPTION: an example of a confidential note tag

Chapter Five:
How to Create Notes

Field Description

Category Tag

Source of Note Information

!CREMATION is an example of a public note tag.

you may specify if confidential notes are to be included or not.

- **Exclamation Point (!) for Public Notes —** When you specify that notes are to be printed on reports or included in a GEDCOM file, notes with an exclamation point as the first character will always be included. However, for printed reports you may opt to print only notes containing an exclamation point at the beginning, which will exclude confidential and personal notes. (See the charts at the end of this chapter.) Use this form of notes for details that you will want to be published in a public report, such as a book or on the Internet.
- **No Character for Personal Notes —** If you do not use a significance character at the beginning of a note or do not tag the note at all, it will always be printed when you specify that notes are to be printed but do not specify that only public notes be printed. They will always be included in a GEDCOM file if you request notes to be included. See the tables at the end of this chapter. This form of note is useful for making notes to yourself, such as reminders, actions to take, or conflicts to resolve.

Category Tag

This is a keyword or words that identify the event, lineage, subject, or research tag for the entry. Enter the tag in all capital letters followed by a colon. When more than one tag word applies, separate them with a hyphen (-) and end the tag with a colon. When a single tag contains more than one word, such as adult christening, use the underscore character to separate the words (*ADULT_CHRISTENING*).

Exception should be made for the prefixes *HALF* and *STEP*, where the use of a hyphen is recommended. See Table 5-1 for a list of standardized tag words for use in note documentation. The tags in Table 5-1 are listed by major categories that help to select the appropriate note for each entry. *Event tags* are used to supplement documentation for genealogy events. Normally, events will be documented in source templates. *Lineage tags* are used to note information about relationships that do not involve source references. *Subject tags* are used to document information not covered by the normal source templates. *Research tags* should be used for noting further investigation required to complete the documentation for an individual. The last column lists tags for the convenience of those who wish to add supplementary LDS event documentation.

Source of Note Information

Usually a note contains relevant information that you wish to maintain in your database. It may be a note indicating that two different sources

Table 5-1: Recommended Note Tags

Event	Lineage	Subject	Research	LDS Events
ADOPTION	CHILD	BIOGRAPHY	ACTION	BAPTISM
BIRTH	CHILDREN	CEMETERY	AKA (also known as)	BLESSING
BURIAL	BROTHER	CENSUS	COMMENT	CONFIRMATION
CHRISTENING	FATHER	CITIZENSHIP	CONFLICT	DEACON
CREMATION	HALF-(relative)	COURT	DEADEND	ELDER
DEATH	MOTHER	EDUCATION	ERROR	ENDOWMENT
DIVORCE	PARENTS	HONORS	FILE	HIGH_PRIEST
EMIGRATION	SIBLINGS	HOSPITAL	NAME (variations)	MISSION
IMMIGRATION	SISTER	LAND	NIL (nothing located)	PATRIARCHAL_ BLESSING
MARRIAGE	SPOUSE	MEDICAL	NOTE (more info)	PRIEST
NATURALIZATION	STEP-(relative)	MILITARY	PLACE	SEALING_PARENTS
PROBATE		OBITUARY	QUESTION	SEALING_SPOUSE
		OCCUPATION	RESEARCHER	SEVENTY
		ORGANIZATIONS	UPDATE	TEACHER
		RELATIONSHIP		
		RELIGION		
		RESIDENCE		

contain conflicting information about an event, or it may simply be an event that is not covered by a PAF source entry. The source details should include enough information so that someone else can easily locate the material. You may specify any or all of the following: title, years covered, source identification, volume, publication date and place, pages, and repository where the information is located.

Main Details or Information

After the source of the material is specified, enter the information to be documented. Your description should be brief, but at the same time it should contain sufficient detail to be unambiguous. Avoid using incomplete sentences, abbreviations, or terminology that is likely to be unfamiliar to others. The following example would probably confuse many users:

Date unkn. MIA at Somme. nil.

Recommended Note Tags

The more appropriate entry might be:

> !DEATH: Date is unknown. No documentation has been located. Family tradition holds that John Baxter was declared missing in action after the Second Battle of Somme, France. The battle took place during World War I, 21 Mar. 1918.

Once the official documents that verify the family tradition or that correct the tradition have been located, this note should be replaced by an appropriate entry in the source documentation screens.

The above note may be accompanied by an ACTION note that indicates what efforts have been made to locate the military records, so that others will not waste time making the same efforts.

A blank line will terminate the note and separate it from subsequent notes. If a note requires more than one paragraph, do not include a blank line between the paragraphs, or they will be treated as a different note.

Good notes contain the name of the individual about whom the information is recorded, so that the information can be meaningful if it is extracted into another program and then is separated from the correct PAF record. It should not contain a RIN or MRIN number, since those record identification numbers are relevant only to your own database.

Multiple Tags

When you need to document an item that contains information about more than one event or topic, you should enter multiple tags separated by hyphens. The tags should be ordered by their significance in the entry.

For example, consider a newspaper article that makes a reference to an honor and a family relationship. Since there is no concrete information in this reference about a death date or place, this item is more likely to be a note, rather than a source. In your notes for the individual, you might make the following entries:

Multiple note tags are hyphenated.

> !HONORS-CHILD: "A University Honors Donors", New York Times; Film NYT-1344;25 Apr 1906; Section A, page 25; Santa Clara County Public Library, Los Altos, California. This article is about Harvard University donors and mentions Charles W. Finley. The award was accepted by a surviving son, Albert Finley, but does not mention a death date or place.
>
> ACTION: Search the archives of Harvard University donors for a possible death date of Charles W. Finley.

Since the article is primarily about an honor and the child is a secondary mention, the order of the tags should be the HONORS tag, followed by the CHILD tag.

Note: The above entry could be entered as a general source citation for the son, Albert, as documentation for the relationship to his parents, especially if nothing more significant is available to document the relationship.

Using the Notes Selector Feature

The Notes Selector feature is designed to help manage your notes, but it can cause frustration if you are not aware of how it functions. Essentially, it is a feature that allows you to only display the notes with specific note tags on your screen based on a selection criteria, or filter. When you wish to enter the notes screen, it will first display the Notes Selector window as shown below.

Notes Selector window

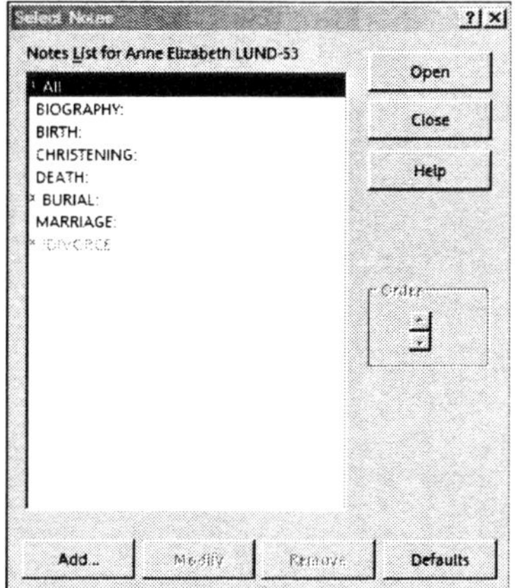

You must indicate which notes you wish to see by selecting the tag from the scroll window. All other notes are ignored while you work on the notes for that tag. You may edit any of the notes for the selected tag, or if you enter a new note in the screen for a selected tag, it will automatically tag the note for you.

Add Note Tag window.

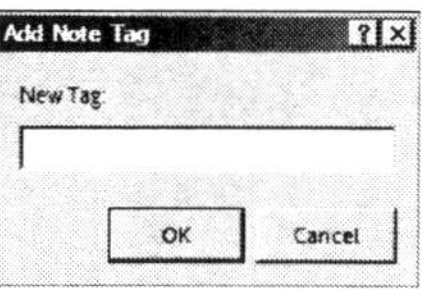

Whenever there is a tagged note in your notes screen, the corresponding tag in the Notes Selector window will be flagged with an asterisk (*). A few standard note tags are always included in the Notes Selector window, including a tag representing *All* notes.

You may add new tags to the list by clicking on the *Add* button. When the Add Note Tag window appears, enter the name of the tag along with the desired Notes Significance Character, if needed. You need not enter the colon at the end of the tag.

The Notes Selector feature does not work with Marriage record notes.

Keep in mind that the Notes Selector feature considers a tag with a significance character different from the same tag without a significance character. For example, the tag *~ADOPTED* is different from the tag *!ADOPTED*, which is different from the tag *ADOPTED*. The default tags in the Note Selector window do not contain significance characters. If you use the Notes Selector feature and find that notes you expect to appear are missing, it is usually because the tag you selected does not contain the significance character you used when creating the note.

Also, if you have notes with tags that do not normally appear in the window, PAF will automatically add them to the list and display them in a shaded color. The shaded tags will not be included in the Notes Selector window for other individuals.

You can change the order of the tags in the scroll window using the *Up* and *Down* arrows at the right side of the Notes Selector window. Highlight the tag to be moved and click one the arrows to move it up or down.

Turning the Notes Selector Feature On or Off

The Note Selector feature is toggled on and off in the *Preferences* option of the *Tools* pull down menu. Select the *General* tab at the top of the window to display the window shown below:

In PAF 4, the Display Notes Selector boxes are on the left side of the General Preferences window.

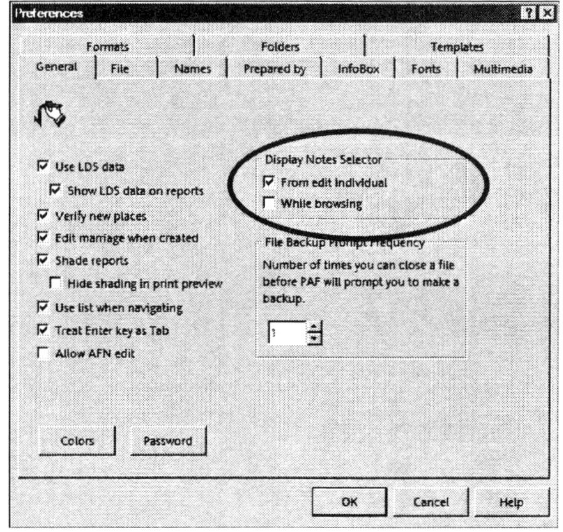

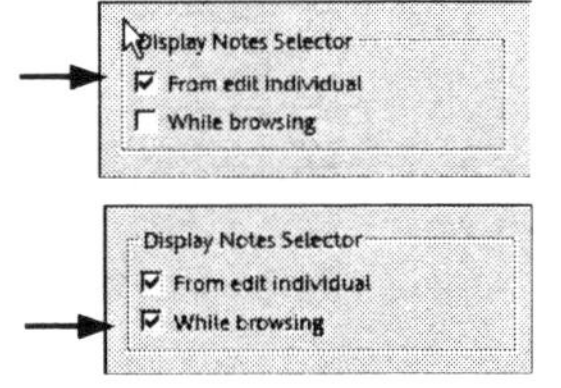

Check the *Display Note Selector* boxes to activate the feature, or check them off to turn the feature off. The *From Edit Individual* box specifies that the Notes Selector window will appear when you click on the *Notes* icon from the Edit Individual window. The *While Browsing* box specifies that the Notes Selector window will appear when you use the *Notes* option in the *Edit* pull down menu or the *Notes* icon on the toolbar without having an Edit Individual window open.

Specifying Notes Options for Reports

When a report or chart has the option to include notes, the specification of which notes to include or exclude is found on the *Print Reports* option of the *File* pull-down menu. Each report or chart has a slightly different options window, but they all work the same way. The one that follows is taken from the Family Group Record window and shows the choices available for controlling which notes are printed on reports.

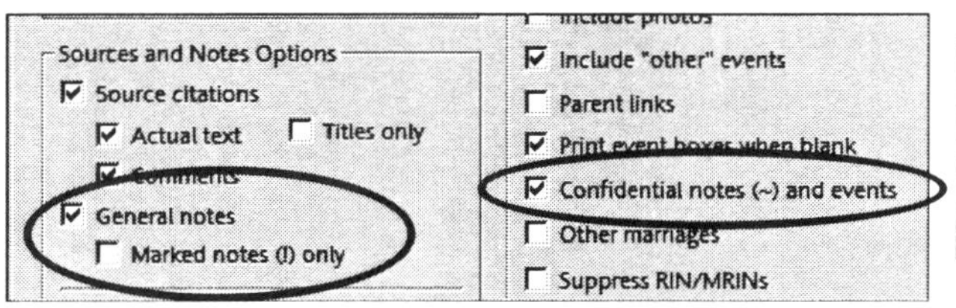

Boxes for controlling which notes are printed on reports.

There are basically three types of notes, as described at the beginning of this chapter: Public (!), Confidential (~), and Personal (no character, nc). To help understand how to use the three check boxes, follow the table below.

The four options for printing notes in reports.

Table 5-2: Setting Options for Notes in Printed Reports

General Notes	Marked Notes (!) Only	Confidential Notes (~)	Results
Not checked	Not available	Checked or not checked	No notes are printed
Checked	Not checked	Not checked	All notes except Confidential (~) notes are printed
Checked	Checked	Checked or not checked	Only Public (!) notes are printed
Checked	Not checked	Checked	All notes are printed

Specifying Notes Options for GEDCOM files

When creating a GEDCOM file from the *Export* option of the *File* pull-down menu, the option window contains the following two choices: Notes and Confidential data.

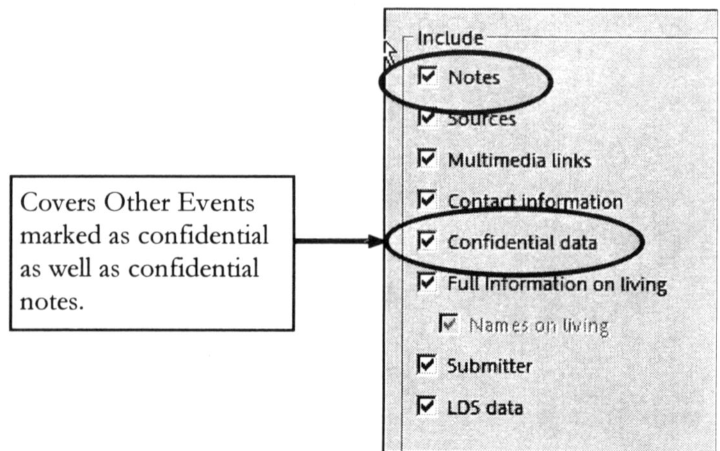

The following chart will help determine how to specify which notes to include in a GEDCOM file.

Table 5-3: Setting Options for Notes in GEDCOM Files

Notes	Confidential data	Results
Checked	Not checked	All notes except confidential notes are included
Checked	Checked	All notes are included
Not checked	Checked or not checked	No notes are included

Chapter Six: Tagged Note Entries

This is the generic syntax for tagged note entries:

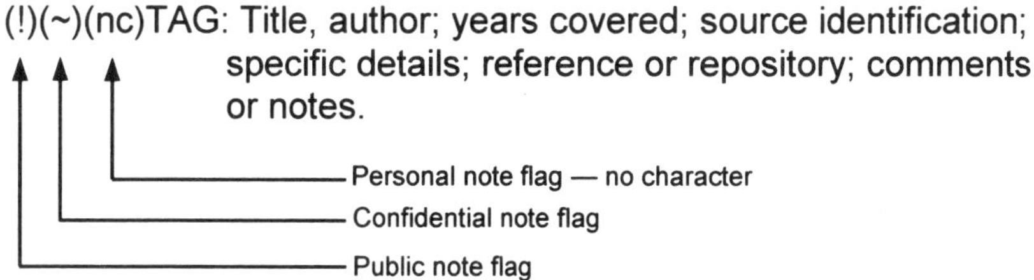

Use this general format for Note entries.

Table 6-1: Examples of Tagged Note Entries

Documentation	Typical Circumstance	Note Entry
Book, Bible, Pamphlet, Periodical, Journal (published)	Passage in the source references a family residence. Documenting this item will aid future research on possible family members.	RESIDENCE: *The Hydes of Virginia; 1843-1860*, Johnson, Clyde; Richmond, Virginia, Fremont Press, 1987; page 104; Sutro Library, San Francisco, California. The passage mentions that Charles R. Hyde owned a home in Ashland, Hanover, Virginia.
Cemetery Record	Ownership of a burial plot recorded, but no record of burial.	CEMETERY: Centennial Cemetery Accounts, Gooding, Richard; 1948-50; Centennial Cemetery, Salt Lake City, Utah; page 35, plot 145-4. Entry records the purchase of two burial plots by Charles R. Miller on 5 May 1948, but records show someone else buried in them.
Census Record	Entry in census mentions family members without names or ages.	CHILDREN: Census, Virginia, Fairfax Co.; 1840 U.S Federal; M704 number 558;p.103; National Archives, San Bruno, California. Entry for John Birchwood lists 3 males, 15-20 years, 1 male 20-30 years, 1 female 20-30 years.
Church Record	Entry in parish records indicates membership but contains no genealogy data. Dates of entries are illegible.	RELIGION: St. Matthew's Lutheran Church Membership Records, 1946-1948; page 28, line 17; Oakland, California. The entry indicates that Paul Harrison was a member and served as a deacon.
Citizenship Record	Certificate of citizenship on record; birth date known, documented with a source.	CITIZENSHIP: Buergerbuch (citizen records); Leipzig (Sachsen), Stradtrath, 1501-1892; item 1, 12 Feb 1878; Upper Hutt, New Zealand Family History Center, FHL film 1441549.

Notes usually relate to details that are tangential to the genealogical facts of an individual, such as birth, marriage and death.

Chapter Six:
Tagged Note Entries

General Rules for Choosing Notes instead of Source Entries

General Rules for Choosing Notes instead of Source Entries

- Typically, use notes for biographical information such as residences and physical characteristics, and use source entries for such items as births, marriages, deaths, and evidence of familial relationships.
- Use notes when the item refers to an action by the researcher, supplemental information, undocumented comments or traditions, research notes, or non-genealogical information.

Notes can often contain information that will help locate vital genealogical details at a later time.

Deciding where to put some information is often a matter of personal preference.

Documentation Item	Typical Circumstance	Note Entry
City Directory	Directory mentions occupation and place of business.	!OCCUPATION: City Directory; Cape Town, South Africa; 1857; page 96; Cape Town Public Library, South Africa. Entry lists Joseph Brody in business as a cobbler with a shop at 67 Broad Street, Cape Town.
Court Record	Transfer of land title showing place of residence.	!RESIDENCE: Court Proceedings; Sussex County, Delaware; 1897; Vol. 17, page 34; County Court, Georgetown, Delaware. Entry lists transfer of parcel of land at Parson's Hill to Harold Randall on 7 Aug. 1897.
Database	Notes for an individual extracted from the Pedigree Resource File.	!MEDICAL: Pedigree Resource File; LDS Church, CD-ROM; dated 5 Sep 1999; disk 4; Info submitted by Hugh Brunell. Note extracted for Joshua Livingston: "Joshua Livingston died of consumption."
Family Records	Family records indicate that a person was known by a different name.	!NAME: Personal Correspondence; Knowles, Randall; 13 May 1867; Letter written by Peter Knowles to his son William. The salutation refers to William as "Billy."
Index Record	Index of land records lists transfer of homesteaded plot.	!LAND: Homestead Index, Douglas County, Kansas; 1868-1875; Vol 6, page 49, line 9; County Recorder's Office, Lawrence, Kansas. Record shows that Noah Smith recorded plot 45-ST-16 under the 1847 Homestead Act.

Documentation Item	Typical Circumstance	Note Entry
Land Record	Copy of deed of sale in family records.	!LAND: Deed of Sale; 1848; Jacob Lynch to Robert Nielsen; 23 Jan 1848; County Recorder, Parke County, Indiana; Plot No. J5456-14. Photocopy in possession of Jacob Hansen, Bedford, Indiana.
Military Record	Regimental discharge records indicate physical disability.	!MILITARY-MEDICAL: British Military Discharge Archives; 1798-1800; Film HO-567-34, frame 67, 5 Dec. 1798; Discharge of Harold Minor, Corporal, 18 years of service in Kings 15th Regiment. Photocopy in possession of Neville Hudson. Discharge due to lame right leg.
Newspaper Article	Article describes event pertaining to a relative.	!OCCUPATION: "Farm accident injures Paxton Farmer", Ford County Weekly Journal; Vol. 5, 14 Jun. 1903, page 2; Periodical Room, Ford County Library, Paxton, Illinois. Robert Adler Esler was severely injured when a steam tractor exploded.
Oral Interview	Interview contains numerous anecdotes concerning family history.	!BIOGRAPHY: Interview; Holden, James; 2 Jan 1985; by grandson James Holden III at St. George, Utah; transcript in possession of James Holden, Las Vegas, Nevada.
Passenger List	Passenger list shows the arrival of a family, indicating the date and ship's name.	!IMMIGRATION: *Lists Of Inhabitants Of Colonial New York*; O'Callaghan, Edmund Bailey; Chapter 7, Early Immigrants to New Netherland 1657-1664; page 78; Jonas Bartelsz, wife and two children 3 and 4 years old arrived at New York City on *De Vergulde Bever* (The Gilded Beaver) on 29 Mar 1660.
Private Correspondence	Biographical information mentioned in a letter among some family records.	!EDUCATION-MILITARY: Hansen Family Correspondence, 1841-1843; Letter from John Schmitt of Boston, Massachusetts, to Sally Hansen in Chicago, Illinois; letter dated 4 Jun 1843; Correspondence in possession of Peter Hansen, Amarillo, Texas; Letter indicates that Noah Hansen, Sally's father, was a surgeon for the U.S. Army and that he was trained at the State University of New York at Brockport, New York.

Chapter Six: Tagged Note Entries

Research notes are best listed in the Notes section so that they can be viewed together on the same screen.

Documentation Item	Typical Circumstance	Note Entry
Tax List	Residence of an individual is established by reference in a tax roll.	!RESIDENCE: Anderson County Tax List, 1801; Clinton, Anderson County, Tennessee; FHL Film 373492, page 3; Charles Page is listed as paying a $3.17 tax assessment on 6 Jul 1801.
University Record	Enrollment records from a university document the education of an individual.	!EDUCATION: Westminster College Class Rolls, 1867; Fulton, Missouri; Vol 7, page 11, line 14; Registrar's Office, Fulton, Missouri; Entry for James Grant indicates that he is enrolled in a history curriculum.
Vital Record—Court Record	Court record indicates the settlement of a dispute between two brothers over the division of property in a business failure.	!COURT: Ada County Court Record; 1947-1950; County Judicial Archives, Boise, Idaho; ACR Film 235, frame 17; photocopy in possession of Harold Poulsen, Lewiston, Idaho; item records the court mandated settlement of assets between brothers Isaac Poulsen and Jacob Poulsen on 5 May 1948.
Vital Record - Police Report	Police record reports an unsolved missing person case.	!NOTE: Flint City Police Records; 1978; Flint, Michigan; City Records Dept., City Hall; Vol 3, page 67, 7 Mar 1978; Report indicates that Sharon Gates was reported missing by her mother, Sylvia Gates, on 25 Feb 1978. The case was never resolved.
Research Note	A personal reminder to continue searching for the will for an individual.	RESEARCH: Prerogative Court of Canterbury; Book 13, Page 56; 1834; Need to continue searching the wills in Berkshire County for references to James Milward Harris.
Conflict	Details in a shipping record hint that an individual died at sea 18 months prior to the date of death. Further research is needed to validate the information.	!CONFLICT: *Peril at Sea*; Howard, Jonathan; 1798; London Book Sellers; page 56; British Library, London, England; Commentary indicates that George Moreland was captain of the frigate *Shepherd's Quest* when it sank in a storm on 23 Mar 1797. Death records documented in sources show death on 14 Oct 1795.

Chapter Seven: Considerations for PAF 3.x

The PAF 3.x program contains a Source and Note documentation system that is similar to that of PAF 4, but does not include some of the Windows capabilities that PAF 4 supports.

The Source Description screen shown below is used for adding and editing your source entries.

```
                  SOURCES FOR THE BIRTH OF JOSIAH TINGEY
Source Description
   Source Title:
   Author:
   Publication Information:
   Source Call Number:
   Source Comments (Press F3 to add/edit):
   Repository Name:
         Address:


       Telephone:
Individual Reference
   Film/Volume/Page Number:
   Date of Entry:
   Actual text (Press F3 to add/edit):
   Comments (Press F3 to add/edit):
Esc=Cancel   F1=Save   F6=Source List   F8=Ditto   F9=New   Alt+H=Help
             F2=Remove PgDn=Next Source PgUp=Previous Source
```

The PAF 3 Source Description and Individual Reference screen

PAF 3.x does not have a field for Actual Text in the Source Description. The Individual Reference field (same as Citation Detail field in PAF 4) contains only an Actual Text field. Source Description comments, Individual Reference Actual Text, and Individual Reference Comments are displayed, added, and edited by highlighting the specific line and pressing F3. The corresponding screen is displayed as shown below:

```
------SOURCE DESCRIPTION COMMENTS------
Name:
Event:



Esc=Cancel      F1=Save                                  Alt+H=Help
```

Note: All screen illustrations in this chapter are taken from PAF 3.

Chapter Seven: Considerations for PAF 3.x

The PAF 3.x Source List is shown below.

The Source List screen in PAF 3.x

```
                    SOURCE LIST FOR JOSIAH TINGEY

Ancestral File: CD-ROM; 1992
Ancestral File: FamilySearch.org
Census: 1880 U.S. Federal, Utah, Washington County
Cape Town Mail: South Africa, Cape Town
Family Records: Belnap, Amos Kay
Family Records: Jensen, Melbourne and Elva Smith
Family Records: Lund, Anne
History of Stonington: Connecticut, 1649-1900
International Genealogical Index: FamilySearch.org
Parish Record: England, Suffolk, Debenham; 1688-1690
Personal Knowledge: Smith, Harold James
Research Report: Rands—3689

↓↑=Move   Enter=Select   Esc=Cancel   Print   Delete   searcH   Alt+H=Help
```

PAF 3.x cannot include images of documents or multimedia files. PAF 3.x does not allow the use of italics or parentheses.

PAF 3.x does not have the same options for printing records or including sources. The only choice is whether to print the full source description, source title only, or no source description for every person on the family group sheet. However, if you choose the full source description, you have three choices for which comments to print: all comments, those marked with an exclamation point (!), or no comments. PAF 3.x does not allow the use of the tilde (~) for confidential note tags.

Printing options for the Source List in PAF 3.x

```
                        SOURCE LIST OPTIONS

        Sources to print (F=Full Source or T=Title only) :   F
   -if full source: (A=All comments, !=Those marked, =None):   A
                        Pages to print — Beginning page :   1
                                          Ending page : 999

Esc=Cancel              F1=Continue                Alt+H=Help
```

The Individual Summary record offers the same choices as PAF 4.

Merging Source Descriptions

PAF 3.x allows you to automatically and manually merge source descriptions. You do this by pressing **T** (ma**T**ch) and choosing *Merge Sources, Sources.* Then choose *Manually merge.*

The information that PAF uses to find matching source records is the source title and call number. The repository name is used to find matching repositories.

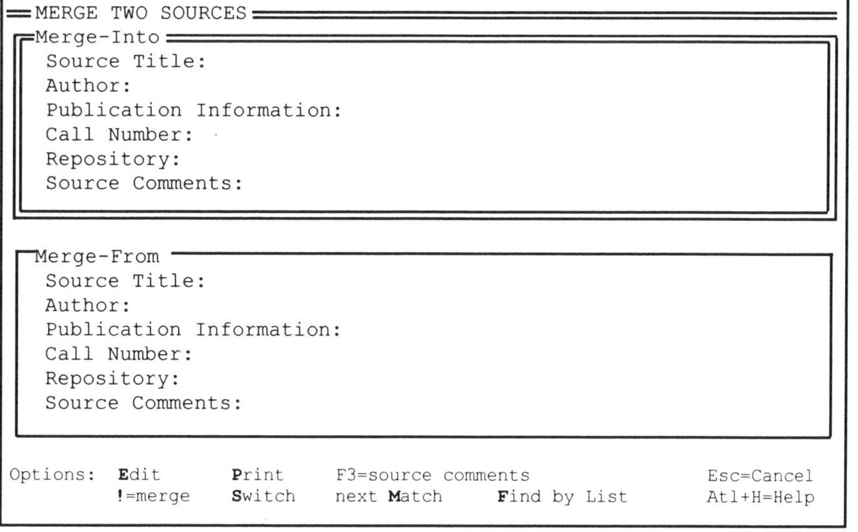

The PAF 3.x source merging screen

The source entry at the bottom is merged into the source entry at the top.

PAF 4 and PAF 5 allow you to merge only identical source descriptions. It is done automatically, and the user has no control. The number of sources and repositories merged is displayed.

Chapter Eight: Data Entry Guidelines for Names

Proper data entry of individual names and place names is important for good documentation. Haphazard practices will reduce the effectiveness of many of the PAF program's search tools and will make printed reports confusing. The following recommendations will help make your information more universal.

Guidelines for Proper Names

Proper names are always entered using the Edit Individual window. In the versions prior to PAF 5, the given names (first and middle) are entered in the top field and the surname in the second field below as shown below.

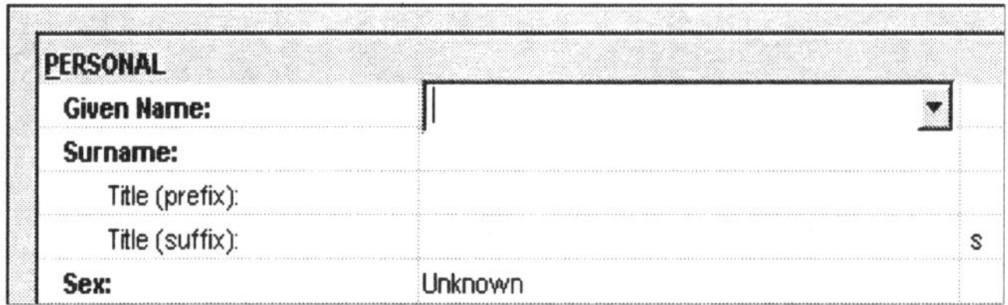

Name fields in the Edit Individual window for versions prior to PAF 5

PAF 5 introduced a new method for entering names, designed to allow flexibility for a variety of name formats. Users in cultures that specify the surname before the given names, or that use double surnames, may now set their PAF program to handle their naming custom as the default format. As shown in the figure below, PAF 5 provides a single field for the entire name, rather than having separate fields for each component of an individual's name. When an individual's name is entered, the PAF program automatically scans the components to identify the given names, the surname, and, when present, the suffix title.

The name field in the Edit Individual window for PAF 5

If the normal sequence of names in your database does not have given names first, followed by the surname and a suffix title, then you may change the scanning rules in the Preferences window as described later in this section. (See Changing the Name Order.)

After PAF 5 has scanned the name for its component parts, it will display the results for you to verify that it is correct. For example, when you enter a name such as:

William Henry McKinley Jr

the program will change it to appear as follows:

William Henry /McKinley/ Jr

with the surname enclosed in slash marks. A window will appear to allow you to correct errors as follows:

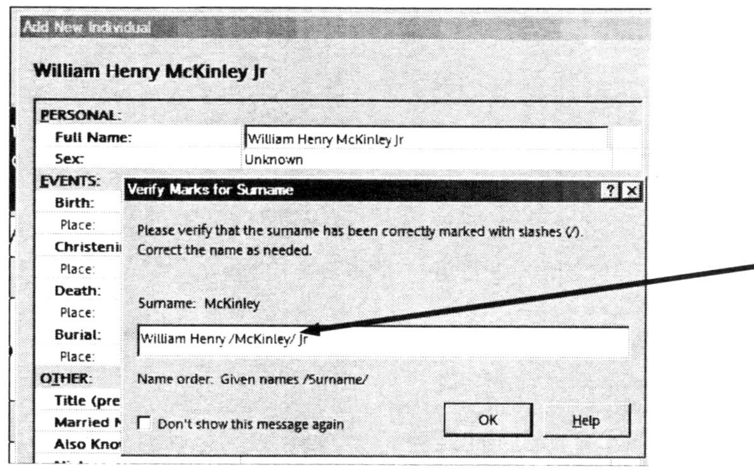

The slash marks specify which name the program has identified as the surname.

The name will appear without the slash marks in all other windows and reports as it has in previous versions of PAF. Do not try to remove the slash marks or you will prevent the program from properly storing the name in your database and sorting it in lists or reports.

If you wish to skip the verification step for your names, you may turn it off in the Preferences window, or by checking the box *Don't show this message again* in the window above. If the name you are entering does not conform to the scanning rules you have chosen, you may enter the slash marks in the name field yourself to override the scanning process.

You may turn off the verify step to save time.

Suggestions for Given Names

Most of the time, dealing with given names is not difficult. However, problems occur when the given names are unknown, when names change because of migration to a new country, or when a nickname appears in genealogical records. When the given names are not known, do *not* enter "unknown". Just leave the space blank. When given names are known, the best approach is to enter all given names (including diacritical marks).

Never enter the word unknown as a proper name or place name.

Chapter Eight: Data Entry Guidelines for Names

If more than one name is possible, enter them separated by *or*. For example:

Maria or Mary /Price/

Names of royalty pose a special problem for which establishing a consistent rule is difficult. We recommend that names of countries or large provinces should not be used as surnames. For example, enter a name of a child of a royal family that does not have a formal given name as:

Gisela of France //

This will cause the name to appear elsewhere as:

, Gisela of France

Even though PAF includes a Nickname field and an Also Known As field at the bottom of the window, the program you use might not include these fields in reports or in GEDCOM files. The Focus/Filter search features of PAF make it possible to search name fields for records that *contain* the search name, allowing you to select records with a variety of names in the given name field. Keep in mind that your data may be shared with others whose software has different features.

Avoid entering a person's occupation in a name or title field.

When given names have changed during someone's lifetime, we recommend entering the name used last as the first one in the field, followed by other names separated with *or*. For example, if an individual was given the name Tiago at birth, then later emigrated and changed his name to James, we suggest that the given name be entered as follows:

James or Tiago

Someone known widely by a nickname might be entered as follows:

Elizabeth or Lizzie

Enclosing names in quotes or parentheses is not necessary. It also is not necessary to include misspellings or slight variations unless they are so unusual that they must be shown for clarification.

Suggestions for Surnames

Since the surname generally is used to sort records for lists, the method for entering surnames is more important. When you enter a surname, consider where it should appear in an alphabetical list. When names have changed during the individual's lifetime, enter the family name given at birth, including diacritical marks. If possible, document details that confirm the name change. Do not enter surnames in all capital characters, as PAF can be set to print and display surnames in all capital letters automatically for you.

It is best to not enter surnames in all capital characters.

If over the course of time the surname was changed completely, such as a new name given when a person emigrated, consider entering the new name after the birth name, separated by *or*. For example, an individual born with the name of McCoullogh changed his name upon immigrating, enter the information as follows:

McCoullogh or Coolley

The change should be documented with a source citation that validates the name change. Sometimes descendents alter their surname by dropping diacritical marks or adopting a popular variation on the name. Such changes might be reflected using the correct birth name, with the new variation listed after the word *or*. For example:

Hålvørsen or Alvorsen

Once the new surname has become the name given to children at birth, the original name is no longer necessary in the surname field. The decision to use this format might depend on how different the two names are. However, in any case, it is important to document when the change became commonly used.

In PAF 5, you will probably find it convenient to denote the surname by entering the slash marks yourself when the surname contains more than one element. For example, the above example should be entered as follows:

Harold /McCoullogh or Coolley/

If you enter the slash marks yourself, PAF 5 will not ask for verification.

otherwise, the program will only specify Coolley as the surname.

As suggested above, avoid using names of countries or major provinces as surnames for royalty. However, if a royal family has established the name of their estate as a well known family name, then it is appropriate to specify it as the surname. For example:

Aldegarde d' /Aunay/

Other name fields in the Edit Individual window.

OTHER:
Title (prefix):
Married Name:
Also Known As:
Nickname:

If you enter the slash marks yourself, PAF 5 will not ask for verification.

Suggestions for Titles

Enter Titles if they were used to distinguish an individual or if they make it easier to identify an individual when many generations used the same given name. The prefix title field in PAF 5 has been moved down to the OTHER section of the Edit Individual window, and the suffix title has become part of the name field. In earlier versions, the title fields are located below the surname field.

Care must be taken when entering a suffix title in PAF 5 because the scanning process will not always recognize a suffix title and may interpret it as the surname. Do not enter occupations in the title field. Use the Notes screen or a Source entry. The following table lists titles and their common abbreviations for assistance in research. Most religious, military, and royalty titles are Prefix Titles. Relationship titles are usually Suffix Titles.

Frequently used titles and abbreviations

Table 8-1. Titles and Their Common Abbreviations

Relationship		Religious		US Military		Royalty/Official	
Junior	Jr	Archbishop	Abp	Admiral	Adm	Alderman	Esquire—Esq
Senior	Sr	Bishop		Airman	Amn	Ambassador	Governor– Gov
the Second	II	Cardinal	Card	Captain	Capt	Baron	Judge
the Third	III	Deacon	Dea	Colonel	Col	Baroness	King
the Fourth	IV	Elder		Commander	Cmdr	Baronet	Lord
the Fifth	V	Monsignor	Msgr	Corporal	Cpl	Congressman	Marchioness
the Sixth	VI	Pastor		Ensign	Ens	Count	Marquis
Esquire	Esq Esq.	Pope		General	Gen	Countess	President– Pres
PhD	PhD	Rabbi		Lieutenant	Lt Lieut	Czar	Prince
Doctor	MD M.D. DDS D.D.S.	Reverend	Rev	Major	Maj	Czarina	Princess
twin		Vicar		Midshipman	Midn	Doctor– Dr	Queen
				Petty Officer	PO	Duchess	Representative-Rep
				Private	Pvt	Duke	Senator– Sen
				Seaman		Earl	Sir
				Sergeant	Sgt	Emperor	Sir Baron
				Warrant Officer	WO	Empress	Sir Knight

Suffix Titles are underlined.

Suffix Titles are underlined in the table above. The use of *twin* as a suffix title is optional. Using *twin* as a title can help avoid mistakes in a Match/ Merge when the names of the twins are very similar.

The name scanning process in PAF 5 will automatically recognize a few suffix titles, including *Sr*, *Sr.*, *Jr*, *Jr.*, *Second*, *II*, *Third*, *III*, *IV*, *V*, *VI*, *Esq*, *Esq.*, and *Esquire*. For example, if you enter a name as follows:

William Henry McKinley Jr

the PAF 5 program will change it to appear as:

William Henry /McKinley/ Jr

If you wish to enter a suffix title that is not automatically recognized, you will need to enter the slash marks yourself. For example, the name:

William Henry McKinley Rev.

Must be entered as follows to prevent *Rev.* from being designated as the surname:

William Henry /McKinley/ Rev.

A complete list of the suffix titles recognized by PAF 5 is shown below.

Sr	Sr.	Jr	Jr.	II
Second	III	Third	IV	V
VI	PhD	MD	M.D.	DDS
D.D.S.	Esq	Esq.	Esquire	

The suffix titles that are automatically recognized by PAF 5.

Changing the Name Order

PAF 5 allows you to change the default name scanning process to allow variations in the sequence that names are identified. In the Preferences window, select the Name tab to display the following screen:

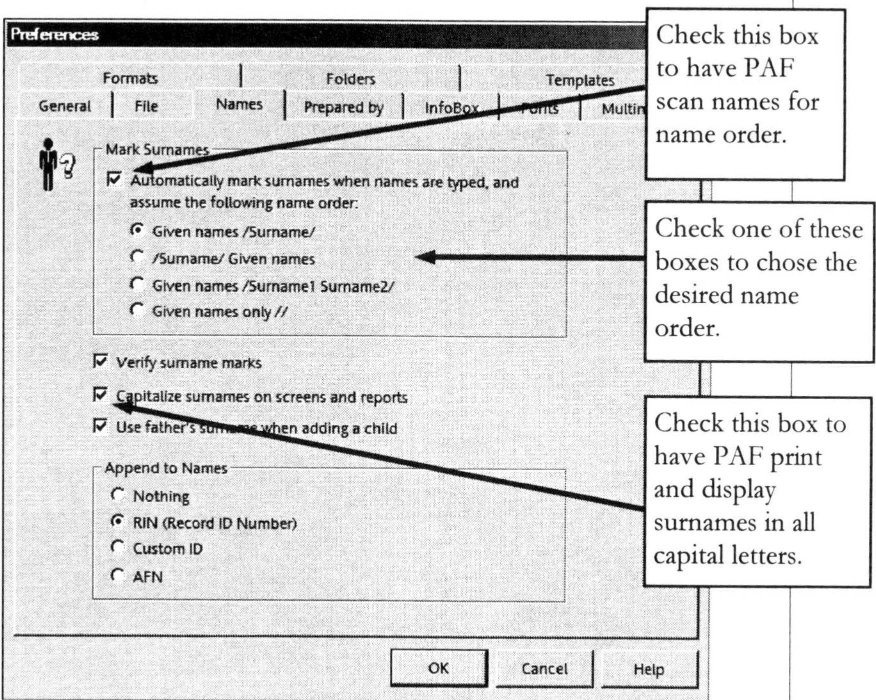

Chapter Eight: Data Entry Guidelines for Names

In the Mark Surnames box you can chose to have PAF automatically scan the names to identify the components. If you turn off this feature, you will be required to enter the slash marks yourself to delineate the surname.

There are four alternatives for name order. If you select the automatic scanning feature, you must select the one that will best identify your typical name order. You may always override the option you specify by entering the slash marks yourself when entering a name in the Edit Individual screen. We recommend that you specify the automatic scanning process to reduce the possibility for error.

Guidelines for Place Names

The format for place names changed dramatically when PAF 3 was released. Instead of four separate fields for the various levels of a place name, PAF 3, and subsequently PAF 4 and PAF 5, combined the separate fields into a single field and allowed the use of a comma to separate the levels.

All four levels of a place name are entered in a single field, separated by commas.

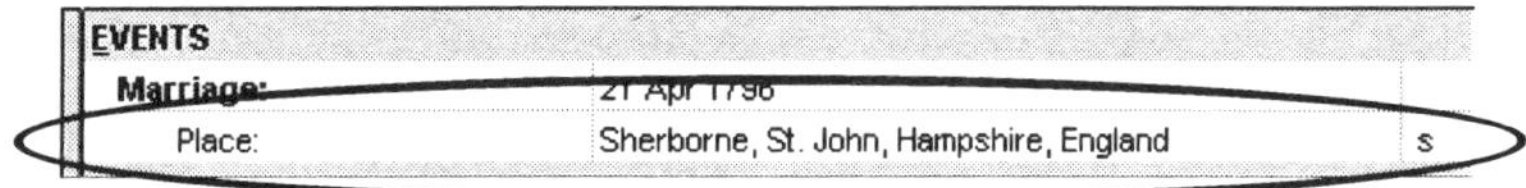

This important improvement gives greater flexibility for entering place names, especially if one or two of the names are particularly long. We suggest the following guidelines to improve the consistency of your data and your ability to search the place name fields using the Focus/Filter feature.

In spite of the fact that each event has only one place name field, PAF still functions with four levels, as follows:

- Level 1: City, parish, borough, village, town, etc.
- Level 2: County, shire, district, etc.
- Level 3: State, province, country (if not state)
- Level 4: Country, empire, kingdom, etc.

Place names in a position beyond the fourth level are only searchable using the Search Focus/Filter feature by using the *Contains* search criteria on the Full Place name.

Ascending Order

Enter place names from left to right in ascending order of significance. In other words, enter the city or parish name first, followed by the county or shire, and then the state, province, or country (when no state is involved). In some cases the fourth level will be the name of the country.

The currently accepted policy is not to enter *USA* as the country name, except when necessary to distinguish between country names that are the same as U.S. state names, such as Georgia. Be careful not to allow preceding blanks in front of names. PAF will insert appropriate blanks in locations when displaying them on the screen or printing them on reports.

Missing Place Names

If part of the place name is unknown, do not enter the word *unknown.* Rather, include the comma as if the place name were there, but leave the name blank. For example, if the city or parish where the event occurred is unknown, use:

, New London, Connecticut

Often the name of the county is the same as the city, and the comma at the beginning will indicate that the city is not known.

Avoiding Abbreviations

Since there are many ways to abbreviate place names, avoid using abbreviations whenever possible. *NSW* is not obvious to everyone as being New South Wales. The U.S. state codes MO, ME, MI, MA are confusing and easily mistaken. Also, punctuation for abbreviations is inconsistent. A few abbreviations are widely used, such as *St.* or *Ste.* for *Saint.* Do not use *Mt.* for *Mountain.* For example, enter *St. George*, but do not use *Mt. View* for Mountain View. All other abbreviations should be avoided. Exceptions are rare and include such names as Washington, D.C., and Mexico, D.F. If you use an abbreviation, always enter a period and a space after the abbreviation.

Exceptions for abbreviations are rare:
Mt.— Mount
St.— Saint
Ste.— Sainte
D.C.— District of Columbia
D.F.— Distrito Federal

Descriptive Words

Avoid using adjectives, adverbs, or prepositions with a place name. When they are necessary, separate them from the location by a comma. For example, the entry *of Charleston* will not be selected when you search for *Charleston* because it is stored in your database as a different place. When such descriptive words are used, separate them with a comma. For example, enter *of, Charleston.* This technique has the advantage of reducing the search trees inside the PAF software, thus speeding up the search time and making your searches more comprehensive. Usually you should place the descriptor (in this case, *of*) in the first position of the place name field.

Note: If not separated by commas, descriptive words will impact the order of names in the Place-Name report.

Minimize the number of descriptive words used in place names and do not capitalize them, to avoid possible confusion with the location's name.

It's best to use only the these terms and use them sparingly.

The following list of descriptive words should suffice:

and
at sea
between
near
now
of
or
probably

For example, descriptive words might be used as follows in the Birth Place field for someone born on the road:

between, Groton, New London, Connecticut, and, Stonington, New London, Connecticut

A search using the Focus/Filter search features allows searching on each level or the Full Place name.

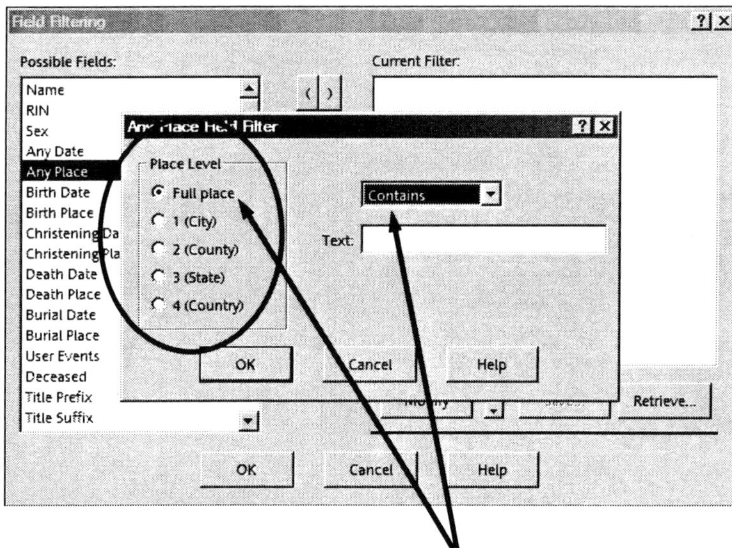

Place names beyond the fourth level will be selected only when the *Contains* search criterion is used on the Full Place name.

It is good practice to consider the limitations of searching the data when entering place names. For example, the phrase at sea, near, Madagascar, Africa will yield a better search result than at sea near Madagascar, Africa.

Using the Official Name

Enter the official name of the place where the documentation of an event is recorded For example, enter the parish name, rather than the name of the town, if a baptism or marriage is documented in parish records. LDS members may wish to enter the name of the ward or stake as well as the town where the event was documented in order to prevent confusion when there are duplicate place names in the same region. For example:

Brighton Ward, Salt Lake City, Salt Lake, Utah

However, you should try to minimize entries in the place name field that shift the components to a higher level. Such a practice reduces the effectiveness of a Focus/Filter search on the place name fields.

Try to minimize entries that shift names to a higher level.

If the event is known to have occurred in an unusual place, enter the details in the Notes. For example, a baptism in a lake, river, or creek should be entered as a note. The name of the hospital where a birth occurred, or the name of a cemetery should be entered in the notes. Otherwise, the Place-Name report will be confusing.

Place Name Changes

When the name of a place has changed since the date of the event being documented, use a consistent nomenclature that will provide clarity and facilitate searching. For example, enter the official name of the place at the time of the event, followed by the current name, separated by the word *now* using commas.

Kariba, Rhodesia, now, Zimbabwe

Stargard, Pomerania, Prussia, now, Poland

Independent Cities

When cities are not part of a county, enter the name of the city in the level designated for county with the word *city* to indicate that it serves as the county designation. For example:

St. Louis, St. Louis (city), Missouri

Independent cities should be designated by adding the word *city* in county level.

Conversion of Abbreviations

We recommend converting all place-name abbreviations in older documentation to the corresponding full name, such as U.S. state names, counties, and countries.

England versus Great Britain versus United Kingdom

We recommend the use of the more specific location names of *England*, *Scotland*, *Ireland*, *Wales*, *Isle of Man*, and *Channel Islands*, rather than the more general terms of *Great Britain* or *United Kingdom.*

Appendix:

Common Abbreviations

U.S. State and Territory Postal Codes

Canadian Province Postal Codes

Appendix: Common Abbreviations

The following tables are included to assist with research in documents that contain common abbreviations. Now that field lengths are not a limiting factor, it is no longer necessary to use abbreviations in your database. However, it is still important to use consistent spelling for place names so that name searches will be exhaustive.

These tables are based on the most recent lists available from searches on the Internet. As time passes, we recommend that you check for more recent listings on the Internet.

Table A-1: U.S. State and Territory Postal Codes

AL	Alabama	ID	Idaho	MT	Montana	RI	Rhode Island
AK	Alaska	IL	Illinois	NE	Nebraska	SC	South Carolina
AZ	Arizona	IN	Indiana	NV	Nevada	SD	South Dakota
AR	Arkansas	IA	Iowa	NH	New Hampshire	TN	Tennessee
CA	California	KS	Kansas	NJ	New Jersey	TX	Texas
CZ	Canal Zone	KY	Kentucky	NM	New Mexico	UT	Utah
CO	Colorado	LA	Louisiana	NY	New York	VT	Vermont
CT	Connecticut	ME	Maine	NC	North Carolina	VA	Virginia
DE	Delaware	MD	Maryland	ND	North Dakota	VI	Virgin Islands
DC	District of Columbia	MA	Massachusetts	OH	Ohio	WA	Washington
FL	Florida	MI	Michigan	OK	Oklahoma	WV	West Virginia
GA	Georgia	MN	Minnesota	OR	Oregon	WI	Wisconsin
GU	Guam	MS	Mississippi	PA	Pennsylvania	WY	Wyoming
HI	Hawaii	MO	Missouri	PR	Puerto Rico		

Table A-2: Canadian Province Postal Codes

AB	Alberta	NB	New Brunswick	NT	Northwest Territories	PQ	Quebec
BC	British Columbia	NF	Newfoundland	ON	Ontario	SK	Saskatchewan
MB	Manitoba	NS	Nova Scotia	PE	Prince Edward Island	YT	Yukon

Table A-3: Great Britain County Abbreviations

These abbreviations cover England, Scotland and Wales. They are used by the LDS Family History Library for cataloging and sorting. There are other standard abbreviations such as the three-letter Chapman Codes, and the 1813 Key to the Ancient Parish Registers of England and Wales.

Abbr	County	Abbr	County	Abbr	County
ABER	Aberdeen	ESSX	Essex	ORKN	Orkney
ANGL	Anglesey	FLIN	Flint	OXFO	Oxford
ANGU	Angus	GLAM	Glamorgan	PEEB	Peebles
ARGY	Argyllshire	GLOU	Gloucester	PEMB	Pembroke
AYR	Ayr	HAMP	Hampshire	PERT	Perth
BANF	Banff	HERE	Hereford	RADN	Radnor
BEDF	Bedford	HERT	Hertford	RENF	Renfrew
BERK	Berkshire	HUNT	Huntingdon	ROCR	Ross & Cromarty
BERW	Berwick	INVE	Inverness	ROXB	Roxburgh
BREC	Brecknock / Brecon	IMAN	Isle of Man	RUTL	Rutland
BUCK	Buckingham	KENT	Kent	SELK	Selkirk
BUTE	Bute	KINC	Kincardine	SHET	Shetland / Zetland
CAER	Caernarvon	KINR	Kinross	SHRO	Shropshire (Salop)
CAIT	Caithness	KIRK	Kirkcudbright	SOME	Somerset
CAMB	Cambridge	LANA	Lanark	STAF	Stafford
CARD	Cardigan	LANC	Lancashire	STIR	Stirling
CARM	Carmarthen	LEIC	Leicester	SUFF	Suffolk
CHAI	Channel Islands	LINC	Lincoln	SURR	Surrey
CHES	Cheshire	LOND	London (Middlesex)	SUSS	Sussex
CLAC	Clackmannan	MERI	Merioneth	SUTH	Sutherland
CORN	Cornwall	MDSX	Middlesex (London)	WARW	Warwick
CUMB	Cumberland	MLOT	Midlothian	WLOT	West Lothian
DENB	Denbigh	MONM	Monmouth	WMOR	Westmoreland
DERB	Derbyshire	MNTG	Montgomery	WIGT	Wigtown
DEVO	Devonshire	MORA	Moray	WILT	Wiltshire
DORS	Dorsetshire	NAIR	Nairn	WORC	Worcestershire
DUMF	Dumfries	NORF	Norfolk	YRKS	Yorkshire
DUNB	Dunbarton	NHAM	Northampton		
DURH	Durham	NOTT	Nottingham		

Table A-4: Country Abbreviations and Internet Codes

The country abbreviations listed below are the standard codes used by the LDS Family History Library. The two-digit Internet codes are listed to help identify the country of origin for e-mail messages.

Abbreviation	Country	Internet Code
AFRICA		
ALGR	Algeria	DZ
ANGO	Angola	AO
BENI	Benin	BJ
BOPH	Bophuthatswana (So. Africa)	
BOTS	Botswana	
BUFA	Burkina Faso	BF
BURU	Burundi	BI
CABI	Cabinda	
CAMR	Cameroon	CM
CAFR	Central African Republic	CF
CHAD	Chad	TD
CISK	Ciskei (So. Africa)	
....	Congo (see Zaire)	CG
CONR	Congo (Kinshasa)	
....	Cote d'Ivoire (see Ivory Coast)	CI
DJIB	Djibouti	DJ
EGYP	Egypt	EG
EQGU	Equatorial Guinea	GQ
ERIT	Eritrea	
ETHI	Ethiopia	ET
GABO	Gabon	GA
GAMB	Gambia	GM
GHAN	Ghana	GH
GUIN	Guinea	GN
GIBI	Guinea-Bissau	GW
IVCO	Ivory Coast	CI
KNYA	Kenya	KE
LESO	Lesotho	LS
LIBE	Liberia	LR
LIBY	Libya	LY
....	Madagascar	MG
MALW	Malawi	MW
MALI	Mali	ML
MRTA	Mauritania	MR
MORO	Morocco	MA
MOZA	Mozambique	MZ
NAMI	Namibia	NA
NIGE	Niger	NE
NIGA	Nigeria	NG
RWAN	Rwanda	RW
ST&P	Sao Tome & Principe	ST
SENE	Sengal	SN
SILE	Sierra Leone	SL
SOMA	Somalia	SO
SAFR	South Africa	ZA
SUDA	Sudan	SD
SWAZ	Swaziland	SZ
TANZ	Tanzania	TZ
TOGO	Togo	TG
TRAN	Transkei (So.Africa)	
TUNI	Tunisia	TN
UGAN	Uganda	UG
VEND	Venda	
WALV	Walvis Bay	
....	Western Sahara	EH
ZAIR	Zaire	ZR
ZAMB	Zambia	ZM
ZIMB	Zimbabwe	ZW
ARCTIC ISLANDS		
....	New Siberian Islands	
....	North Land Island	
....	Sakhalin Islands	
....	Wrangel Island	
ATLANTIC ISLANDS		
ACSH	Ascension Island (UK)	
AZOR	Azores (Portugal)	
BERM	Bermuda (UK)	BM
....	Bouvet Island (Norway)	BV
CANI	Canary Islands (Spain)	
CVIS	Cape Verde Islands	CV
FAER	Faeroe Islands (Denmark)	FO
FALK	Falkland Islands (Malvinas)	FK
MADI	Madeira Islands (Portugal)	
STHC	Saint Helena Colony	SH
....	South Georgia Islands (see Falkland Islands)	FK
SSAN	South Sandwich Islands (UK)	
....	Svalbard and Jan Mayen Islands	SJ
TRIS	Tristan de Cunha Islands	
ASIA		
AFGH	Afghanistan	AF
ASTL	Australia	AU
BAHR	Bahrain	BH
BANG	Bangladesh	BD
BHUT	Bhutan	BT
BRUN	Brunei	BN
BURM	Brunai (Myanmar)	MM
CAMB	Cambodia (see Kampuchea	KH
SRIL	Ceylon (see Sri Lanka)	LK
CHIN	China	CN
CYPR	Cyprus (Republic)	CY
CTUR	Cyprus (Turkey)	
....	East Timor	TP
HOKO	Hong Kong	HK
INDR	India	IN
INDO	Indonesia	ID
IRAN	Iran	IR
IRAQ	Iraq	IQ
ISRA	Israel	IL
JAPA	Japan	JP
JORD	Jordan	JO
CAMB	Kampuchea (see Cambodia)	KH
KAZA	Kazakhstan	KZ
KORN	North Korea	KP
KORS	South Korea	KR
KUWA	Kuwait	KW
KYRG	Krygyzstan (Kirgistan)	KG
LAKS	Lakshadweep Islands (India)	
LAOS	Laos	LA
LEBA	Lebanon	LB
MACA	Macao (Portugal)	MO
MALY	Malaysia	MY
MONG	Mongolia	MN
BURM	Myanmar (see Burma)	MM
NEPL	Nepal	NP
OMAN	Oman	OM
PAKI	Pakistan	PK
PHIL	Philippines	PH
QATR	Qatar	QA
SAAR	Saudi Arabia	SA
SING	Singapore	SG
SRIL	Sri Lanka	LK
SYRI	Syria	SY
TADZ	Tadjikistan (Tadzhilistan)	TJ

ASIA (continued)
TAIW .... Taiwan .... TW
THAI ..... Thailand .... TH
TRKY .... Turkey .... TR
TRKM ... Turkmenistan .. TM
UAEM ... United Arab Emirates .... AE
UZBK .... Uzbekistan .... UZ
VIET ..... Vietnam .... VN
YEMN ... Yemen .... YE

CARIBBEAN ISLANDS
ANGU ... Anguilla .... AI
ANBA ... Antigua and Barbuda .... AG
ARUB ... Aruba .... AW
BAHA ... Bahamas .... BS
BARB ... Barbados .... BB
CAYM ... Cayman Islands. KY
CUBA ... Cuba .... CU
DOMI .... Dominica .... DM
DOMR .. Dominican Republic .... DO
GREN ... Grenada .... GD
GUAD ... Guadeloupe & St. Martin Is. ... GP
HAIT ..... Haiti .... HT
JAMA .... Jamaica .... JM
.... Leeward Islands
.... Lesser Antilles
MART ... Martinique .... MQ (French)
MSER ... Montserrat .... MS
NAVA ... Navassa Island
NEAN ... St. Maarten and Netherlands Antilles .... AN
PURI ..... Puerto Rico .... PR (U.S.)
STCN ... St. Kitts and Nevis Islands .. KN
STLU .... Saint Lucia LC
STVG ... St. Vincent and Grenadines VC
TR&T .... Trinidad and Tobago .... TT
T&CI ..... Turks and Caicos Islands .... TC
VIGB ..... Virgin Islands .... VG (U.K)
VIUS ..... Virgin Islands .... VI (U.S.)
WEIN .... West Indies
.... Windward Islands

CENTRAL AMERICA
BELZ .... Belize .... BZ
CORI .... Costa Rica .... CR
ELSA .... El Salvador .... SV
GUAT ... Guatemala .... GT
HOND .. Honduras .... HN
NICA .... Nicaragua .... NI
PANA ... Panama .... PA

EUROPE
.... Aegean Islands
ALBN ... Albania .... AL
ANDO .. Andorra .... AD
ARMR .. Armenia .... AM
ASTR ... Austria .... AT
AZER ... Azerbaijan .... AZ
BALE .... Belearic Islands (Spain)
BELA .... Belarus .... BY
BELG ... Belgium .... BE
BERE ... Beresan (Russia)
BESS ... Bessarabia (Moldavia-Ukraine)
BOSN ... Bosnia-Herzegovina ..... BA
BUKO ... Bukovina
BULG ... Bulgaria .... BG
CHAI .... Channel Islands(UK)
GB .... Great Britain ..... GB
CIS .... Commonwealth of Independent States (former USSR)
.... Corsica (France)
.... Crete (Greece)
GLUK ... Gluckstal (Russia)
GROA .. Croatia .... HR
CZEC ... Czechoslavakia. CS
CZER ... Czech Rebublic. CZ
DENM .. Denmark .... DK
ENGL ... England .... UK
ESTO ... Estonia .... EE
FINL ..... Finland .... FI
FRAN ... France .... FR
GEOR .. Georgia .... GE
GERM .. Germany .... DE
GIBR .... Gibraltar (UK) .... GI
GREE ... Greece .... GR
HOFF ... Hofnungstal (Russia)
HUNG .. Hungary .... HU
ICEL ..... Iceland .... IS
.... Ionian Islands (Greece)
IREL ..... Ireland .... IE
IMAN .... Isle of Man (UK)
ITAL ..... Italy .... IT
KUTS ... Kutschurgan (Russia)
LATV .... Latvia LV
LIEC ..... Liechtenstein LI
LITH ..... Lithuania .... LT
LUXE ... Luxembourg ..... LU
MACE ... Macedonia .... MK
MALT .... Malta .... MT
MEDS ... Medieval States Sub-Region (Europe-Near East before 1500)
MOLD ... Moldava .... MD
MOLO ... Molotschna (Russia)
MONA ... Monaco .... MC
MNEG ... Montenegro (Cnra Gora)
MRUP ... Mariupol (Russia)
NCAU ... North Caucasus (Russia)
NETH .... Netherlands ..... NL
.... Netherlands Antilles .... AN
NIKO ..... Nikolayev (Russia)
NIRE ..... Northern Ireland
NORW .. Norway .... NO
ODGR ... Odessa/ Grossliebental
POLA .... Poland .... PL
PORT ... Portugal .... PT
ROMN .. Romania .... RO
RUSS ... Russia .... RU
SAMA ... Samara (Russia)
SARA .... Saratov Volga
SMAR ... San Marino ...... SM
.... Sardinia (Italy)
SCHW .. Schwedengebiet (Russia)
SCOT ... Scotland (UK) ..
SERB .... Serbia
.... Sicily (Italy)
SLVK .... Slovak Republic. SK
SLVN .... Slovenia .... SI
SPAI ..... Spain .... ES
.... Soviet Union .... SU
SVAL .... Svalbard (Norway)
SWED ... Sweden .... SE
SWIT .... Switzerland ...... CH
UKRA ... Ukraine .... UA
UK .... United Kingdom UK
VATI ..... Vatican City ...... VA
VOLH .... Volhynia (Russia-Poland)
WALE ... Wales (UK)
.... Yugoslavia .... YU (see BOSN, SERB, SLOV, CROA, MACE, MNEG)

INDIAN OCEAN ISLANDS
ANDA ... Andaman Islands (India)
BIOT ..... British Indian Ocean Territory (UK).. IO

INDIAN OCEAN ISLANDS *(continued)*

.... Chagos Archipelago (same as BIOT)
.... Cocos (Keeling) Islands CC
COMO .. Comoros Is. ...... KM
CROZ ... Crozet Island (French)
.... Diego Garcia Island
.... Heard & McDonald Islands .... HM
.... French Southern Territory .... TF
KERG ... Kergulen Islands (French)
MADA ... Madagascar ...... MG
MALD ... Maldives .... MV
.... Mascarene Islands
MTUS ... Mauritius .... MU
MAYO ... Mayotte .... YT
NICO .... Nicobar Islands (India)
PEIS ..... Prince Edward Islands (So. Africa)
REUN ... Reunion .... RE (French)
SEYC ... Seychelles .... SC
SOCO ... Socotra Islands (Yemen)

NORTH AMERICA

ACAD ... Acadia (historically, Nova Scotia)
CAN...... Canada .... CA
GRNL ... Greenland .... GL
MEXI .... Mexico .... MX
STPM ... St. Pierre & Miquelon (French) .... PM
USA...... United States .... US

PACIFIC ISLANDS

AMSA ... American Samoa (USA) .... AS
.... Caroline Islands (Fed. States of Micronesia)
CHRI .... Christmas Islands (Australia) CX
CLIP ..... Clipperton Island
COCO .. Cocos (Keeling) Islands CC
COOK ... Cook Islands ..... CK
EASI ..... Easter Island
.... Ellice Islands (Tuvalu)
FSMI ..... Federated States of Micronesia .... FM
FIJI .... Fiji .... FJ
FLIN ..... Flint Island (USA)
FRPO ... French Polynesia (France) .... PF
.... Galapagos Islands (Ecuadaor)
.... Gambier Islands (French Polynesia) ..... PF
.... Gilbert Islands (Kiribati)
GUAM .. Guam (USA) ... GU
.... Hawaii (USA)
JARV .... Jarvis Island (USA)
JOHN ... Johnston Atoll (USA)
JUAN .... Juan Fernandez Islands (Chile)
KERM ... Kermadoc Islands (New Zealand)
KING .... Kingman Reef (USA)
KIRI ...... Kiribati Islands.. KI (Line Islands - US)
KURI ..... Kuril Islands (Russia)
.... Leeward Islands (French)
MARQ .. Marquesas Islands (French)
MARI .... Marshall Islands .... MH
.... Melanesia
.... Micronesia ...... FM
MIDW ... Midway Islands (USA)
NAUR ... Nauru .... NR
NCAL .... New Caledonia (French) .... NC
NZEA .... New Zealand .. NZ
NIUE ..... Niue .... NU
.... Norfolk Island (Australia) ..... NF
NOMA .. Northern Marianas (USA) .... MP
PALA .... Palau .... PW
PALM ... Palmyra Island (USA)
PANG ... Papua New Guinea .... PG
.... Phoenix Islands (Kiribati)
PITC ..... Pitcairn Islands (UK) .... PN
.... Polynesia
.... Samoan Islands
.... Society Islands (French)
SOLI ..... Soloman Islands.SB
TOKE ... Tokekau Islands.TK
TONG ... Tonga .... TO
TTPI ..... Trust Territories of the Pacific Islands (USA)
TUAM ... Tuamotu Archipelago (French)
.... Tubuai Islands (French)
TUVA ... Tuvalu .... TV
VANU ... Vanuatu .... VU
WAKE ... Wake Island (USA)
WA&F ... Wallis and Futuna (French) .... WF
WSAM .. Western Samoa .... WS
.... Windward Islands (French)

SOUTH AMERICA

ARGN ... Argentina .... AR
BOLI ..... Bolivia .... BO
BRAZ ... Brazil .... BR
CHIL ..... Chile CL
COLM ... Columbia .... CO
ECUA ... Ecuador .... EC
FRGU ... French Guiana .... GF
GUYA ... Guyana .... GY
PARA ... Paraguay .... PY
PERU ... Peru .... PE
SURI .... Suriname .... SR
URUG ... Uruguay .... UY
VENE ... Venezuela ..... VE

WORLD REGIONS

AFRI ..... Africa
ANTA ... Antarctica ...... AQ
ARCT ... Arctic Islands
ASIA ..... Asia
ATIS ..... Atlantic Islands
ATSE .... At Sea (unspecified location)
CARI .... Caribbean Islands
CEAM ... Central America
INOI ...... Indian Ocean Islands
NOAM .. North America
PACI ..... Pacific Islands
SOAM ... South America
WMIS ... World Miscellaneous (unidentified country)

Table A-5: Country Internet Codes in Alphabetic Order

The country Internet codes are listed to assist you in identifying the source of e-mail messages and Web pages when corresponding with researchers worldwide. For example, an e-mail address, goodresearcher@colibry.za, will belong to a person whose Internet Service Provider is located in the country whose code is ZA, which is South Africa. However, note that some ISPs provide access to their services outside their home country, so that you may find a correspondent whose country code does not correspond to the codes in the table. For example, a person in Mexico can subscribe to aol.com. Do not assume that the country code correctly identifies the origin of a correspondent, especially if it is a .com or .net address. Some countries have combined codes. For example, the code .co.uk is a commercial site (.com) in the United Kingdom UK). For the most recent listing of country Internet codes, see:

http://www.din.de/gremien/nas/nabd/iso3166ma/codlstp1/en_listp1.html

Code	Name
BIZ	Business names
COM	US Commercial
EDU	US Educational
GOV	US Government
INFO	General Information
INT	International
MIL	US Military
NAME	Personal names
NATO	NATO field
NET	Network
ORG	Nonprofit
AD	Andorra
AE	United Arab Emirates
AF	Afghanistan
AG	Antigua and Barbuda
AI	Anguilla
AL	Albania
AM	Armenia
AN	Netherlands Antilles
AO	Angola
AQ	Antarctica
AR	Argentina
AS	American Samoa
AT	Austria
AU	Australia
AW	Aruba
AZ	Azerbaijan
BA	Bosnia-Herzegovina
BB	Barbados
BD	Bangladesh
BE	Belgium
BF	Burkina Faso
BG	Bulgaria
BH	Bahrain
BI	Burundi
BJ	Benin
BM	Bermuda
BN	Brunei Darussalam
BO	Bolivia
BR	Brazil
BS	Bahamas
BT	Bhutan
BV	Bouvet Island
BW	Botswana
BY	Belarus
BZ	Belize
CA	Canada
CC	Cocos (Keeling) Islands
CD	Congo (Democratic Republic)
CF	Central African Republic
CG	Congo
CH	Switzerland
CI	Ivory Coast
CK	Cook Islands
CL	Chile
CM	Cameroon
CN	China
CO	Colombia
CR	Costa Rica
CS	Czechoslovakia
CU	Cuba
CV	Cape Verde
CX	Christmas Island
CY	Cyprus
CZ	Czech Republic
DE	Germany
DJ	Djibouti
DK	Denmark
DM	Dominica
DO	Dominican Republic
DZ	Algeria
EC	Ecuador
EE	Estonia
EG	Egypt
EH	Western Sahara
ER	Eritrea
ES	Spain
ET	Ethiopia
FI	Finland
FJ	Fiji
FK	Falkland Islands (Malvinas)
FM	Micronesia (Federated States)
FO	Faroe Islands
FR	France
FX	France (European Territory)
GA	Gabon
GB	Great Britain (UK)
GD	Grenada
GE	Georgia
GF	French Guiana
GH	Ghana
GI	Gibraltar
GL	Greenland
GM	Gambia
GN	Guinea
GP	Guadeloupe
GQ	Equatorial Guinea
GR	Greece
GS	South Georgia and the South Sandwich Islands
GT	Guatemala
GU	Guam (US)
GW	Guinea Bissau
GY	Guyana
HK	Hong Kong
HM	Heard and McDonald Islands
HN	Honduras
HR	Croatia

Appendix:

Country Internet Codes in Alphabetic Order

Haiti — Zimbabwe

HT...... Haiti
HU...... Hungary
ID....... Indonesia
IE....... Ireland
IL........ Israel
IN....... India
IO....... British Indian Ocean Territory
IQ....... Iraq
IR....... Iran
IS....... Iceland
IT....... Italy
JM...... Jamaica
JO...... Jordan
JP...... Japan
KE...... Kenya
KG...... Kyrgyzstan
KH...... Cambodia
KI....... Kiribati
KM..... Comoros
KN...... Saint Kitts & Nevis Anguilla
KP...... North Korea
KR...... South Korea
KW..... Kuwait
KY...... Cayman Islands
KZ...... Kazakstan
LA...... Laos
LB...... Lebanon
LC...... Saint Lucia
LI........ Liechtenstein
LK...... Sri Lanka
LR...... Liberia
LS...... Lesotho
LT...... Lithuania
LU...... Luxembourg
LV...... Latvia
LY...... Libyan Arab Jamahiriya
MA..... Morocco
MC..... Monaco
MD..... Moldovia
MG..... Madagascar
MH..... Marshall Islands
MK..... Macedonia (former Yugoslav Repub.)
ML...... Mali
MM..... Myanmar
MN..... Mongolia
MO..... Macau
MP..... Northern Mariana Islands
MQ..... Martinique (French)
MR..... Mauritania
MS..... Montserrat
MT...... Malta
MU..... Mauritius
MV......Maldives
MW.....Malawi
MX......Mexico
MY......Malaysia
MZ......Mozambique
NA......Namibia
NC......New Caledonia (French)
NE......Niger
NF.......Norfolk Island
NG......Nigeria
NI........Nicaragua
NL.......Netherlands
NO......Norway
NP......Nepal
NR......Nauru
NT.......Neutral Zone
NU......Niue
NZ.......New Zealand
OM......Oman
PA.......Panama
PE.......Peru
PF.......Polynesia (French)
PG......Papua New Guinea
PH......Philippines
PK.......Pakistan
PL.......Poland
PM......Saint Pierre and Miquelon
PN......Pitcairn
PR......Puerto Rico (US)
PS.......Palestinian Territory (occupied)
PT.......Portugal
PW......Palau
PY.......Paraguay
QA......Qatar
RE......Reunion (French)
RO......Romania
RU......Russian Federation
RW.....Rwanda
SA.......Saudi Arabia
SB.......Solomon Islands
SC......Seychelles
SD......Sudan
SE.......Sweden
SG......Singapore
SH......Saint Helena
SI........Slovenia
SJ.......Svalbard and Jan Mayen Islands
SK.......Slovakia
SL.......Sierra Leone
SM......San Marino
SN......Senegal
SO......Somalia
SR......Suriname
ST...... Sao Tome and Principe
SV...... El Salvador
SY...... Syrian Arab Repub.
SZ...... Swaziland
TC...... Turks and Caicos Islands
TD...... Chad
TF....... French Southern Territories
TG...... Togo
TH...... Thailand
TJ....... Tajikistan
TK...... Tokelau
TM...... Turkmenistan
TN...... Tunisia
TO...... Tonga
TP...... East Timor
TR...... Turkey
TT....... Trinidad and Tobago
TV...... Tuvalu
TW..... Taiwan
TZ....... Tanzania
UA...... Ukraine
UG...... Uganda
UK...... United Kingdom
UM..... U.S. Minor Outlying Islands
US...... United States
UY...... Uruguay
UZ...... Uzbekistan
VA...... Vatican City State
VC...... Saint Vincent and the Grenadines
VE...... Venezuela
VG...... Virgin Islands (British)
VI....... Virgin Islands (U.S.)
VN...... Vietnam
VU...... Vanuatu
WF..... Wallis and Futuna Islands
WS..... Samoa
YE...... Yemen
YT...... Mayotte
YU...... Yugoslavia
ZA...... South Africa
ZM...... Zambia
ZR...... Zaire
ZW..... Zimbabwe

Table A-6: Acceptable Multimedia Formats

Media Type	Description	File Extensions
Photo	Bitmap	.bmp
	Compuserve PNG	.png
	Encapsulated PostScript (EPS)	.eps
	JPEG	.jpg, .jpeg, .jff, .jtf
	PCX	.pcx, .dcx
	Photo CD (Kodak)	.pcd, .fpx
	Tagged Image File Format	.tif
	Windows Metafile	.wmf, .emf
	WordPerfect graphics	.wpg
	Icons and cursers	.ioc, .cur
	DICOM	.dic
	PhotoShop 3.0	.psd
	Truvision TARGA	.tga
	SUN Raster Format	.ras
	Macintosh formats	.pct, .mac, .img, .msp
	LEAD	.cmp
	TIFF CCITT and other fax formats	
Sound	Wave	.wav
	MIDI	.mid, .rmi
Video	Audio/Video	.avi, .mpg, .mpeg, .mov

Table A-7: Frequently Used Source Entries

Source Title: Ancestral File: Web version 4.19 (1999)
Author: LDS Family History Department
Publication Information: Web Site
Call Number: www.FamilySearch.org; accessed [date]
Repository Name: Family History Library
Address: 35 North West Temple, Salt Lake City, Utah 84150
Telephone: 1-801-240-3702
Actual Text:
Comments:

Source Title: Ancestral File: CD-ROM, 1999
Author: LDS Family History Department
Publication Information: CD-ROM: 16 discs plus 4 supplementary discs
Call Number:
Repository Name: Family History Centers—worldwide
Address:
Telephone:
Actual Text:
Comments:

Source Title: International Genealogical Index (IGI): CD-ROM, 1998
Author: LDS Family History Department
Publication Information: CD-ROM: 23 discs plus 6 supplementary discs
Call Number:
Repository Name: [Enter the location where you searched the files]
Address:
Telephone:
Actual Text:
Comments:

The .tif image file format is the most recommended for archiving.

Appendix:

Frequently Used Source Entries

Source Title: International Genealogical Index (IGI): Web Site, 2002
Author: The Church of Jesus Christ of Latter-day Saints
Publication Information: Web Site
Call Number: <www.FamilySearch.org>
Repository Name: Family History Library
Address: 35 North West Temple, Salt Lake City, Utah
Telephone: 1-801-240-3702
Actual Text:
Comments:

Source Title: Pedigree Resource File: 1999
Author: The Church of Jesus Christ of Latter-day Saints
Publication Information: CD-ROM, Set of 9 discs
Call Number:
Repository Name: [Enter your local Family History Center or other repository]
Address:
Telephone:
Actual Text:
Comments: CD-ROM available at all Family History Centers

Source Title: Pedigree Resource File: Web Site, 2002
Author: Church of Jesus Christ of Latter-day Saints
Publication Information: Web Site
Call Number: <www.FamilySearch.org>
Repository Name: Family History Library
Address: 35 North West Temple, Salt Lake City, Utah
Telephone: 1-801-240-3702
Actual Text:
Comments:

Source Title: Census, British: 1841
or: 1841 British Census
or: England: 1841 British Census
Author: British Government
Publication Information: PRO: HO 107/
Call Number:
Repository Name: Family Records Office
Address: 1 Myddelton Street
London, UK EC1R 1UW
Telephone: 0151 471 4800 (certificate enquiries); 0181 392 5300 (other enquiries)
Actual Text:
Comments: Census taken 6 Jun 1841

Source Title: Census, British: 1851
or: 1851 British Census
or: England: 1851 British Census
Author: British Government
Publication Information: PRO: HO 107/
Call Number:
Repository Name: Family Records Office
Address: 1 Myddelton Street
London, UK EC1R 1UW
Telephone: 0151 471 4800 (certificate enquiries); 0181 392 5300 (other enquiries)
Actual Text:
Comments: Census taken 30 Mar 1851

Source Title: Census: 1861 British
or: 1861 British Census
or: England: 1861 Census
Author: British Government
Publication Information: PRO: RG 9/1-623
Call Number:
Repository Name: Family Records Office
Address: 1 Myddelton Street
London, UK EC1R 1UW
Telephone: 0151 471 4800 (certificate enquiries); 0181 392 5300 (other enquiries)
Actual Text:
Comments: Census taken 7 Apr 1861

Source Title: Census, British: 1871
or: 1871 British Census
or: England: 1871 British Census
Author: British Government
Publication Information: PRO: RG 10/1-627
Call Number:
Repository Name: Family Records Office
Address: 1 Myddelton Street
London, UK EC1R 1UW
Telephone: 0151 471 4800 (certificate enquiries); 0181 392 5300 (other enquiries)
Actual Text:
Comments: Census taken 2 Apr 1871

Source Title: Census, British: 1881
or: 1881 British Census
or: England: 1881 British Census
Author: British Government
Publication Information: PRO: RG 11/1-630 or </http://www.FamilySearch.org>
Call Number:
Repository Name: Family Records Office
Address: 1 Myddelton Street
London, UK EC1R 1UW
Telephone: 0151 471 4800 (certificate enquiries); 0181 392 5300 (other enquiries)
Actual Text:
Comments: Census taken 3 Apr 1881

Source Title: Census, British: 1891
or: 1891 British Census
or: England: 1891 British Census
Author: British Government
Publication Information: PRO: RG 12/1-631
Call Number:
Repository Name: Family Records Office
Address: 1 Myddelton Street
London, UK EC1R 1UW
Telephone: 0151 471 4800 (certificate enquiries); 0181 392 5300 (other enquiries)
Actual Text:
Comments: Census taken 5 Apr 1891

Appendix:

Frequently Used Source Entries

The first U.S. Federal census was taken in 1790 and repeated every ten years. The U.S. Census is maintained confidential for 72 years. The 1890 census was mostly destroyed by fire. Some state and territorial census data are available from as early as 1660.

Source Title: Census, U.S. Federal: State name; YYYY [see example below]
or: YYYY U.S. Federal Census: State name
or: State name: YYYY U.S. Federal Census
Author: US Census Bureau
Publication Information: [varies by state]
Call Number:
Repository Name: U.S. National Archives and Records Administration
Address: [See Table A-8]
Telephone:
Actual Text:
Comments:

Source Title: Census, U.S. Federal: California; 1900 [example of standard U.S. Census]
or: 1900 U.S. Federal Census: California
or: California: 1900 U.S. Federal Census
Author: US Census Bureau
Publication Information: Microfilm
Call Number: T623 number 81-116
Repository Name: U.S. National Archives and Records Administration, Pacific Region
Address: 1000 Commodore Drive
San Bruno, California 94066
Telephone: 1-650-876-9009
Actual Text:
Comments:

Table A-8: Frequently Used Repositories

Repository Name:	The Church of Jesus Christ of Latter-day Saints
Address:	50 East North Temple Salt Lake City, UT 84150-3400
Telephone:	1-801-240-2190
Repository Name:	Family History Department
Address:	50 East North Temple Salt Lake City, UT 84150-3400
Telephone:	1-801-240-2190
Repository Name:	Family History Library
Address:	35 North West Temple Salt Lake City, UT 84150
Telephone:	1-801-240-3702
Repository Name:	Family Records Centre (U.K.)
Address:	1 Myddelton Street London, UK EC1R 1UW
Telephone:	0151 471 4800 (certificate enquiries); 0181 392 5300 (other enquiries) (includes the Office for National Statistics and the General Register Office)
Repository Name:	FamilySearch Center
Address:	Joseph Smith Memorial Building 15 East South Temple Salt Lake City, UT 84150
Telephone:	1-801-363-5466
Repository Name:	Library of Congress (U.S.) Local History & Genealogy Reading Room
Address:	101 Independence Ave, SE Washington, D.C. 20540-4720
Telephone:	1-202-707-5537
Repository Name:	Public Records Office (U.K.)
Address:	Ruskin Avenue, Kew Surrey, England TW9 4DU
Telephone:	0181 876 3444
Repository Name:	U.S. National Archives and Records Administration, Headquarters
Address:	7th & Pennsylvania Ave., NW Washington, D.C. 20408
Telephone:	1-202-501-5400
Repository Name:	U.S. National Archives and Records Administration, Pacific Alaska Region
Address:	654 West Third Ave. Anchorage, AK 99501-2145
Telephone:	1-907-271-2441 (serves Alaska)
Repository Name:	U.S. National Archives and Records Administration, Pacific Region
Address:	24000 Avila Road, 1st Floor-East Entrance P.O. Box 6719 (for correspondence) Laguna Niguel, CA 92607-6719
Telephone:	1-949-360-2641 (serves Arizona and Southern California, Clark Co., NV)
Repository Name:	U.S. National Archives and Records Administration, Pacific Region
Address:	1000 Commodore Drive San Bruno, CA 94066-2350
Telephone:	1-650-876-9009 (serves Northern California, Hawaii, Nevada, except Clark County)

Note the change of name for this repository.

Frequently Used Repositories

Repository Name:	U.S. National Archives and Records Administration, Rocky Mountain Reg.
Address:	Bldg. 48. Denver Federal Center West 6th Ave., and Kipling St. P.O. Box 25307 (for correspondence) Denver, CO 80225-0307
Telephone:	1-303-236-0817 (serves CO, MT, ND, SD, UT, WY)
Repository Name:	U.S. National Archives and Records Administration, Southeast Region
Address:	1557 St. Joseph Ave. East Point, GA 30344-2593
Telephone:	1-404-763-7477 (serves AL, FL, GA, KY, MS, NC, SC, TN)
Repository Name:	U.S. National Archives and Records Administration, Great Lakes Region
Address:	7358 South Pulaski Rd. Chicago, IL 60629-5898
Telephone:	1-773-581-7816 (serves IL, IN, MI, MN, OH, WI)
Repository Name:	U.S. National Archives and Records Adm., Northeast Region (Boston)
Address:	380 Trapelo Rd. Waltham, MA 02452-6399
Telephone:	1-781-647-8104 (serves CT, ME, MA, NH, RI, VT)
Repository Name:	U.S. National Archives and Records Adm., Northeast Region (Pittsfield)
Address:	10 Conte Dr. Pittsfield, MA 01201-8230
Telephone:	1-413-445-6885 (microfilm only)
Repository Name:	U.S. National Archives and Records Adm., Northeast Region (NYC)
Address:	201 Varick St. New York, NY 10014-4811
Telephone:	1-212-337-1300 (serves NJ, NY, PR, VI)
Repository Name:	U.S. National Archives and Records Administration, Mid Atlantic Region
Address:	900 Market St. Philadelphia, PA 19107-4292
Telephone:	1-215-597-3000 (serves DE, MD, PA, VA, WV)
Repository Name:	U.S. National Archives and Records Administration, SouthWest Region
Address:	501 West Felix St., Bldg 1 P.O. Box 6216 (for correspondence) Fort Worth, TX 76115-3405
Telephone:	1-817-334-5525 (serves AR, LA, NM, OK, TX)
Repository Name:	U.S. National Archives and Records Administration, Pacific Alaska Region
Address:	6125 Sand Point Way, NE Seattle, WA 98115-7999
Telephone:	1-206-526-6501 (serves ID, OR, WA)
Repository Name:	
Address:	
Telephone:	
Repository Name:	
Address:	
Telephone:	
Repository Name:	
Address:	
Telephone:	

Enter your own often used repositories here.

Table A-9: Useful Internet Web Addresses

Internet sites can appear and disappear without warning, or they can be merged with other sites. The following table is only current as of the printing date. The Silicon Valley PAF Users Group (SV-PAF-UG) maintains an extensive, up-to-date list of helpful Websites online at:

www.svpafug.org/links.html

URL Address	Description
lcweb.loc.gov/rr/genealogy/	Information about the Library of Congress' world premier collection of U.S. and foreign genealogical and local historical publications. The Library's genealogy collection began as early as 1815 when Thomas Jefferson's library was purchased.
searches.rootsweb.com/ ~usgenweb/usearch.htm	National Archives Search Engine by State
www.britishislesgenweb.org/	GenWeb Project for the British Isles (United Kingdom and Ireland). Part of the WorldGenWeb Project
www.census.gov/ prod/2000pubs/cff-2.pdf www.census.gov/ Prod/2000pubs/cff-4.pdf	Online copy of U.S. Census Bureau's *Factfinder for the Nation*, a newsletter containing details about the availability of U.S. Census records and the addresses of National Archive sites
www.cyndislist.com	Cyndi Howell's Web site containing links to more than 174,000 research sites; links are constantly being added.
www.FamilySearch.org	LDS Church's search engine for the IGI, Ancestral File, Pedigree Resource File, and linked family Web sites; free access to the 1880 U.S., 1881 British and Canadian censuses.

Thousands of Web sites are useful for family history research.

Appendix

Useful Internet Web Addresses

URL Address	Description
www.genuki.org.uk/big/	U.K. GenWeb project for England, Ireland, Scotland, Wales, Channel Islands, and Isle of Man
www.hmc.gov.uk/nra/nra2.htm	Search engine for the indices to the U.K. National Register of Archives (NRA)
www.loc.gov	U.S. Library of Congress, Washington, D.C.
www.pro.gov.uk	Public Records Office in Kew, England. Contains many research aids and references; 1901 U.K. censuses online for a minimal charge.
lists.rootsweb.com	A free, general purpose search facility with access to surnames; includes a database search and keyword search feature
www.usgenweb.org or www.usgenweb.org/SS *(replace the SS with the state postal code)*	Access to the individual U.S. State GenWeb projects with information organized by counties
www.worldgenweb.org/	Information about GenWeb projects in many countries; site sponsored by FranceGenWeb
www.ellisisland.org	Ellis Island—U.S. emigration records; free
www.interment.net	Several million cemetery records compiled from over 3500 cemeteries from around the world

Add your most often accessed Web site addresses here.

Additional Documentation References

Acronyms, Initialisms and Abbreviations Dictionary, (3 Vol.), Detroit: Gale Research, 1989.

Chicago Manual of Style, 14th Edition, Chicago: University of Chicago Press, 1993.

Handybook for Genealogists: United States of America, 8th Edition, Logan, Utah: Everton Publishers, 1998.

Lackey, Richard, *Cite Your Sources: A Manual for Documenting Family Histories and Genealogical Records*, New Orleans: Polyanthos, 1980.

Mills, Elizabeth Shown, *Evidence! Citation and Analysis for the Family Historian*, Baltimore: Genealogical Publishing Company, 1997.

New York Times Manual of Style and Usage, New York: New York Times, 1976.

Pence, Richard A., Understanding Sources, Citations, Documentation and Evaluating Evidence in Genealogy, Internet Class Material, www.pipeline.com/~richardpence/classdoc.htm, 1997.

Ritche, M., *Rookie's Guide to Genealogy Research*, Internet Class Material, 31 Lessons, www.acceleratedgenealogy.com/rookie/rookie.htm, retrieved 2000.

Wylie, John, *How To Cite Sources*, Internet site, www.genealogy.com/genealogy/ 19_wylie.html, November 2000.

Notes

If you add useful information to this manual, consider sending it to the *Guidelines* committee:

Richard Rands

guidelines@svpafug.org

Index

Index

Index

Index

Index